GETHSEMANE

Where the Heart is Crushed

Jimmy Foster

ISBN 978-1-64140-418-1 (Paperback)
ISBN 978-1-64140-420-4 (Hard Cover)
ISBN 978-1-64140-419-8 (Digital)

Christian Faith Publishing, Inc.
296 Chestnut Street
Meadville, PA 16335
www.christianfaithpublishing.com

All Scripture quotations, except where otherwise indicated, are from the King James Version

Printed in the United States of America

In memory of
Mark Davis
A great preacher, Bible teacher, and friend.
You are missed.

CONTENTS

Acknowledgments 7

Introduction..9

Prologue 13

Part One: Christ in Gethsemane

Chapter 1. The Place Called Gethsemane 17

Chapter 2. The Mystery of His Nature 28

Chapter 3. The Mystery of His Prayer 37

Chapter 4. What Prompted the Opening of His Prayer?...........46

Chapter 5. What Inspired the Closing of His Prayer? 55

Part Two: Have You Had a Gethsemane?

Chapter 6. Facing a Personal Gethsemane 69

Chapter 7. The Testing of Faith 83

Chapter 8. The Testing of Sorrow..96

Chapter 9. The Call for Service 112

Chapter 10. The Call for Salvation 123

Chapter 11. The Path Out of the Garden 135

Epilogue...145

ACKNOWLEDGMENTS

Thanks to Del Land
for sharing with us his story
and for allowing us to share it with you.

Gratitude is due
to a video called *Lessons from the Olive Press*
which helped direct my thinking.

My deepest appreciation goes to
Rick Probst and Dan Ratcliffe
of *Faith Talk Live* in Atlanta
for allowing me to use part of our radio interview
in this book.
Also for the opportunity
to present my first book to the public.

INTRODUCTION

No night has ever seemed as dark as this. There is the sense of something lurking at the edges of our imagination, as if something sinister is poised to pounce upon us. The rolling storm clouds have carried with it a sense of dread.

The dark clouds begin to part, revealing a full moon which casts its eerie glow across the garden area. The strange effect is heightened by the twisted trunks of the ancient trees that surround a lone figure. There, beside a large rock, a man is kneeling with his head bowed as if under a heavy burden.

The man's hands are raised in a typical Jewish position of prayer. He is speaking in a very low voice, intending his petition to be heard by a certain set of ears. There is, however, an unsettled and distressed tone to his voice. It is as if he is wrestling with forces unseen to our eyes.

With a sudden lurch, the man doubles over, his hands dropping to grasp his stomach, as wave after wave of seemingly unbearable grief wracks his body. For several minutes, his being continues to shudder under this strain.

Finally, his hands still holding onto his stomach, he lifts his head to fix his gaze upon a specific point. It's as if he is looking directly into the eyes of his Father.

His voice now is resolute and more self-assured, as he continues with his supplication. There is still an inner battle going on, but the man has yielded to an inner calm that permeates his very being.

Gradually, the dark clouds once again move to obscure the light from the moon, and the man is hidden from our view.

* * * * *

It may be the most touching picture in scripture.

The image of Christ praying in agony at Gethsemane moves me like few other things do. I can hardly approach the scripture concerning it without feeling an overwhelming sense of awe. Often when I read the passage from the pulpit, I will get choked up.

Gethsemane has become such a familiar part of the passion narrative that I'm not sure we appreciate the depth of what was transpiring there. It is like the recognizable Bible story that too often we read through without stopping to realize the heartrending implications of the passage.

I can remember as a child that behind the pulpit of the Olive Springs Baptist Church, the church our family attended when I was a child, was the reproduction of a painting of Christ praying in Gethsemane. In it, Christ is serenely sitting on a rock with a full moon just breaking through dark clouds. He seems to be overlooking the town of Jerusalem. Somehow that doesn't seem to capture the true weight of the agony Christ felt, and I sometimes wonder if we can comprehend the magnitude of his pain.

When we really examine Gethsemane, we begin to get a picture of the price Jesus paid for our salvation. Our salvation is free for all, but it was not cheap. It cost Jesus dearly.

When I step back and look at this picture in its entirety, I have to ask myself a couple of questions. First, what is there about this scene that makes it so unique?

I believe it is because when we walk into Gethsemane, we are walking across holy ground. Although we are not physically walking into that garden on the night Jesus prayed there, for we are separated by time and distance, we can in our hearts and minds walk in the midst of those olive trees.

What makes this place special are the people and unseen forces arrayed there. At the center is Christ himself. But we also observe the weary disciples, the betrayer leading an armed mob of men, angels who are sent to minister and strengthen the Son of God, and, unrecorded, there must have been the dark forces of Satan sent to torment the Savior. Literally, the heart of Jesus was crushed.

What we dare to gaze upon is the suffering of deity.

The second question I ask myself is, What does this mean to me personally?

I believe that all scripture is inspired by God, and that it is relevant to us in this age. This is not some dry doctrine. All doctrine has a practical application for our lives if we will just look for it.

Everybody, at some point in their lives, will face a situation where their heart will be crushed. Let me be quick to add that we will *never* have to experience anything that approaches the magnitude of what Jesus suffered, but at the time, it will seem that way to the individual. I have not been immune to that in my life. It is a common experience.

In this book, what I would like to do is to walk with you into the garden.

To take this journey, we need to have our hearts open to hear from heaven and to see what God has in store for us.

There will be times when it might seem like I am taking you on a tour of the Holy Land. I do this to help us catch a glimpse of a former time. In fact, when I was in Israel, there were instances where I almost felt like I was transported in time and could see the land as Jesus saw it. I hope that this will give you a feel of what happened there, as it does me whenever I read the scriptures.

At other times, it might seem so personal, that you may feel like I have been looking over your shoulder.

Part one takes a look at Christ in Gethsemane, and tries to see what was transpiring on that dark night. It will be all about Jesus.

Part two will ask the question, "Have you had a Gethsemane?" What is it that might have crushed your heart? This will be about you and me, and how *His* suffering relates to us.

Why should we take this journey?

There are some disturbing trends I see developing in Christianity today. First off, it seems that many churches have been infused with a culture of *entertainment*. With light shows and productions that rival the best that Hollywood can offer, we wonder, *Have we been conformed to the world?* What happened to pure worship?

There is also the tendency to gear everything to make the "seeker" *comfortable*. Often, invitations to come to Christ are no longer extended. There is the effort to make those who attend "feel good about themselves." They may even be told, "This is the best possible world you will live in." Are we making them feel good about themselves while they are still in their sins? Do we make them comfortable on the path to judgment?

Even more disturbing, there seems to be a *universalist view* prevalent today. There seems to be the feeling that everybody will make it to heaven. Whenever a well-known person passes away, we automatically place him in heaven. There have also been some popular books and movies that suggest everyone will be saved or given a second chance after death. If this were so, why was there a need for Jesus to suffer? Why would he experience such a horrible death?

When you walk into Gethsemane and see it as it actually was, it is not entertaining.

If you could have viewed that scene in its intensity, you would have been decidedly *un*comfortable. Nothing calls for *total commitment* from the Christian like hearing Jesus pray, "Not my will, but thine be done." There can be no casual Christianity when confronted with the realization of what he bore for us.

If you could have sensed all that Jesus was taking upon himself, it would have stirred the realization within you that *you need a savior*.

It is not a scene that would appeal to some individuals, but oh, the *benefits* we reap because he was crushed.

When we walk through a soul-crushing experience, there is one who has walked that way before. He knows and understands and can bring comfort to the uncomfortable and the hurting.

Just as he did for me, when I was facing the most difficult experience of my life…

PROLOGUE

Yea though I walk through the valley of the shadow of death, I will fear no evil: for thou art with me...

—Psalm 23:4 (KJV)

Nothing seems quite so final as death. Nothing strikes the heart quite as hard as the death of a beloved family member. Even when you have a long time to prepare yourself, you're never quite ready for it when it happens.

We were all gathered together in the room: my mom, my brother Johnny, his wife Judy, and myself. No one was saying a word. Each one of us were enveloped in our own world of grief, dealing with it as best we could.

Before us, lying on the table where the doctors had tried to revive him, was our hero. Dad was the one we had always turned to for advice, wisdom, or someone to lean on. What do you do when the one you usually turn to is the one leaving?

It had happened just a few minutes before. He wasn't long gone. But there's just something about a body when the soul leaves it. You don't really need to check for a pulse to know that he's just *not there*. The dulled eyes have no sparkle to them. The skin takes on a pallor that says there is no life here. The one you love so dearly no longer inhabits this shell.

Running into his mouth was the tube where they had tried to ventilate him in their efforts to save his life. That tube had so irritated Dad, and he had fought so hard against it during his time in the

ICU, that I found myself thinking, *Couldn't they have at least pulled that out?*

The silence still hung heavy, as we were turning to go. I reached out to brush his hair back off of his forehead. Goodbye, my hero.

My heart was "crushed."

Ever since the day that I had accepted Christ as my Savior, walking with Jesus had been a joy. He had been there to guide me. He had empowered me to preach his gospel. He had carried me through difficult times. He was my "all in all." Whenever I needed grace, it was poured out on me in bucketful.

I needed a special measure of grace this time.

I needed someone who understood.

I needed someone who had been there himself.

My mind wanders back to the Bible stories I am so familiar with searching for that time when Jesus himself felt this kind of devastation. My thoughts take me to a garden in the dark of night. There in my mind's eye, I see Jesus crushed under the load he is carrying.

Can he sympathize? Does Jesus understand what I am experiencing?

I close my eyes and walk into a place called Gethsemane...

PART ONE

Christ in Gethsemane

Then cometh Jesus with them to a place called Gethsemane, and saith unto the disciples, Sit ye here, while I go and pray yonder.

And he took with him Peter and the two sons of Zebedee, and began to be sorrowful and very heavy.

Then saith he unto them, My soul is exceedingly sorrowful, even unto death: tarry ye here, and watch with me.

And he went a little farther, and fell on his face, and prayed, saying, O my Father, if it be possible, let this cup pass from me: nevertheless not as I will, but as thou wilt.

—Matthew 26:36–39 (KJV)

CHAPTER 1

The Place Called Gethsemane

It had to have happened somewhere in this area. If I were to close my eyes, I could almost hear echoes of a former time, a darker time, when the fate of the world was in the balance.

There's just something about walking over the actual ground where a historical event took place. Whether it is some event from American history or one of the many stories in the Bible, actually standing on the ground makes the episode come alive for you.

Particularly when it comes to the Bible, reading the story after striding over the area helps you to visualize it. It just really pops in your mind.

What is it that makes a mere plot of land seem special or sacred? There is nothing unusual about the topography. The rocky ground upon which I stand is not somehow infused with an added dose of the Spirit of God. He inhabits people, not inanimate objects.

Yet, there is no denying that as I stand here there is something stirring within me that can find its way into my eyes.

I come to the realization that what makes this place special is the one who walked here, the one who knelt here, the one who prayed a simple prayer here. It is the monumental nature of that prayer and its possible ramification that hold my heart in such a deep reverence.

I realize that it is not merely the fate of the world that hung in the balance, but, personally, my own salvation was at stake.

The place upon which I stand is called Gethsemane.

It was 1973, and I was nineteen years old. I was on a tour of the Holy Land. This was about three years before I surrendered to the call to preach, and was still seeking God's will for the rest of my life. The tour was headed up by Dr. Gene Winfrey, a "cowboy" preacher (as my grandmother liked to refer to him) from Oklahoma. With several preachers in the group, we were having a grand time.

On this particular day, we were standing in the Garden of Gethsemane, located at the base of the Mount of Olives, right next to the Kidron Valley.

To this day there are olive trees that still produce olives on the grounds. In the garden proper, there are eight ancient-looking, twisted and gnarled olive trees. Among the trees there is a well maintained, manicured-looking path running in straight lines. The gnarled appearance of the trees gives it a very awe-inspiring atmosphere.

Our hosts relate to us that some of these trees are over two thousand years old. If this is true, then some of these trees might have sheltered the Son of God on that night.

Since the time of my trip, there has been a three-year study done by the Italian National Research Council to try to determine the age of these trees. They were able to determine that three of the trees were over nine hundred years old. They were not able to determine the age of the other five trees because of the gnarled condition of the trees and the fact that the trees were hollowed out. So, there is no way to determine specifically if these trees stood during the time of Christ.

They did determine through DNA analysis that the three testable trees came from the same parent tree. I also read of a 1982 University of California study that did radiocarbon dating of some of the ancient root material and determined that it was possibly 2,300 years old.

Even if these were not the exact same trees that stood while Jesus prayed, then they probably sprang from the original trees.

Standing there and looking at them in 1973, it didn't really matter. It seemed like I was seeing the Garden as it actually appeared on that momentous night. Those trees lend such an authentic touch to the scene, that I can't help but ask myself some questions.

What would it have been like if I had been standing here on that night so many years ago?

Would I have been aware of otherworldly forces at play?

Would a shiver have run down my spine?

Our guide is speaking, "The word *Gethsemane* literally means 'olive press' and indicates that there was probably an olive press located in this area."

As we leave this area, our guide takes us to a church beside the garden called The Church of All Nations. It is a feature in this land that wherever there is an important site, someone has built a church over it. Inside we see cordoned off a slab of rock in the floor.

"Tradition holds that this is the rock where Jesus prayed the night before his crucifixion," our guide says. There is no way to really know if this is indeed the specific spot where Jesus prayed or not. Many sites we see on this tour has little evidence to prove that it is the actual site other than "tradition." Other sites, on the other hand, leave little doubt that they are the genuine location. Places such as the house of Caiaphas, the path from Gethsemane to his house, and the location of Gethsemane at the foot of the Mount of Olives are almost assuredly the actual spots.

If I were to close my eyes and listen, could I imagine I was hearing his prayer?

After this, we are taken about one hundred meters to the north through a walkway to a place called the Grotto of Gethsemane, the "Olive Press." It is a cave-like place that (except for some flooring and a couple of altars that give it a chapel feel) is basically unchanged from the time of Christ.

"It is believed that this is the place where the disciples waited while Jesus went to pray. Tradition (there's that word *tradition* again) indicates that this is possibly where Jesus met with Nicodemus at night." In my mind, I try to imagine those familiar words being intoned here, **"For God so loved the world, that He gave his only begotten Son, that whosoever believeth in him should not perish, but have everlasting life."** (Jn 3:16, KJV)

"It is likely here that the olive press was located."

There is some evidence to show this. On the wall behind the right altar, there is a hole where a long wooden beam was fitted.

There are several types of olive presses (such as one that used a large rolling stone) that were in use during Jesus's time. It appears that the type used in Gethsemane was a lever-based press. At the end of the beam were a couple of weighted stones. Underneath the beam was placed the collection of olives in a woven bag with a large stone placed on top of it. The pressure would begin to crush the olives until the oil began to flow out. When the oil ceased flowing, a second stone was placed upon it to increase the pressure. When the second wave of oil ceased, they placed a third stone and continued the process up to five stones.

With all the questions concerning where the exact spot of his agony took place, there is little doubt that this area was Gethsemane. It was somewhere in this area where he knelt at the crossroad of decision and prayed that prayer. With my salvation, and the salvation of all who would believe hanging in the balance, he prayed, **"Father, if it be possible, let this cup pass from me. Nevertheless, not my will, but thine be done."**

It is this prayer that so enthralls me. Of all the things that transpired in the garden, the prayer overwhelms me and draws my attention to what was transpiring there.

Would the Son of God redeem us, or would he allow us to continue in our sin?

I could close my eyes and think that I was listening to those echoes.

* * * * *

The name "olive press" is an appropriate name for the place where all this occurred. For it was here that the heart of Jesus was *crushed.*

The pain he went through was not imaginary. It is hard to imagine the unseen pressures laid upon Jesus that weighed upon him so heavily. It was so great that during this time of stress an angel appeared to give him strength, and he began to sweat drops of blood. (Luke 22:43–44).

Though some would scoff at the idea of sweating drops of blood and try to assign it the status of myth, there is a very real medical condition called hematidrosis. It is extremely rare. So rare, in fact, that you have probably never known anyone with this condition. It occurs when the tiny blood vessels around the sweat glands begin to constrict and then dilate. They do this till they rupture, seeping blood into the sweat glands themselves. This causes literal blood to be sweated out. This condition is caused by *extreme anguish.*

The blood he sweated was an indication of the intensity of his torment.

From the olive press we learn that to reap the benefits of olive oil, the olive itself must be crushed. Likewise, for us to reap the benefits of the Holy Spirit flowing in our lives, *it was essential that the Son of God go through this heartbreaking process.* Without *his* pain, *we* would receive no benefits. Not only would he suffer pain, but, just like with the olive press, there was ever-increasing pressure placed upon Christ.

Consider the example of the olive press. With the addition of each stone in the cultivation of the olive oil, the oil was designated for five different purposes.

The first oil was reserved for the temple. It was used as anointing oil and to light the lamps on the altar.

The succeeding uses corresponded with each stone placed on the olives. Some oil was designated to sell. The remaining oil was used as fuel, medicine, and finally, in the making of soap.

With each "stone" of pressure placed on Christ, it squeezed out blessings that we might take for granted.

Let's take a look at what a few of these blessings were.

First oil to the temple—the blessing of worship

The fact that the first of the olive oil went to the temple demonstrates that our first priority in life should be our relationship with

God. To live a full and complete life, I believe placing God first in our lives is the most important thing we can do. If we get this first thing right, all the other things in our lives will more easily fall into line.

That doesn't mean there won't be difficulties. Anything worthwhile will require a great deal of work. Whether it's relationships with other people, our marriages, family issues, or work-related problems, nothing comes easy. In fact, anything that comes easy probably will not be valued very highly.

When God takes preeminence in our lives, however, we have his guidance to navigate through rough waters.

What we need to realize, however, is that his type of relationship with our creator would not even be possible without the suffering and the sacrifice of Jesus. We can have a relationship with God only because it was purchased and made possible for us.

His heart was "crushed" so that our hearts could be made whole. Because of what he did, I can not only know "about" God, I can know God intimately.

This ability to have a relationship with God is a gift that was provided to us, but one that I am afraid we take for granted. In fact, the vast majority of people in our world give no thought to spiritual matters, or if they do, they pattern their belief according to their own reasoning.

If a person truly gives God first priority in their lives, he might find himself outside the mainstream of society. The society we live in today is not like what our parents grew up in. We live in a world where sin, and even perversion, is accepted as "normal." To try to live your life according to God's standard of righteousness more than likely will place you at odds with some of those around you.

But, oh, the joy to be able to wake up in the morning and spend time with my Lord. How it encourages, strengthens, and blesses me.

It was made possible by what Jesus did.

The second use of oil was

Oil to sell—our basic needs provided

I had lost my job and became a statistic. I was one of millions in our nation looking for work. I had an outstanding resumé, but whenever I went in for an interview and they found out I was sixty years old, I never seemed to get the job.

I went sixteen months without a job, spending time every day trying to find one. Finally, I found one reasonably close to where I lived. It was a matter of timing. The job became available right when I applied, and I began working fairly soon.

During that time of unemployment, God had given me a supernatural peace that everything was going to be okay. He would provide in his timing. There were times that I got a little anxious about it, but generally, I had a calm peace that ruled my heart. God's timing was impeccable, for I found the job right when I needed it.

Not only did he provide that job, but during that entire sixteen months I was able to pay all my bills and pay them on time. In fact, while unemployed, my credit score went up. It was amazing to see God provide.

God does not promise that we will be wealthy, but he will take care of those that are His. Psalm 37:25 (KJV) says, **"I have been young, and now am old; yet have I not seen the righteous forsaken nor his seed begging bread."**

This relationship with God that Jesus made possible for us means that we have a Father who cares for his children. He wants the best for us. That might mean that some of the things we want, God might withhold. Our Father might determine that they are not best for us and that he has a different way.

That's what "living by faith" is all about. We trust him that he knows what is best, and because we belong to him, he gives us oil to sell to provide for our needs.

Oil for fuel—light and guidance

This is a dark world that we live in. If that fact is not apparent, all one has to do is look at the madness that characterizes life today.

The truth is, it was just as dark in Jesus's time. The known world was ruled by the Roman Empire. What was supposedly a cultured and civilized society ruled their conquests with an iron fist. Its government was totalitarian, slavery was a fact of life, and to entertain the masses, they would put on bloody spectacles where men would kill each other in mortal combat. What passed for representation, the Roman senate, was rife with greed and corruption.

Times were as dark as they had ever been. It was into this world that Christ came. Like a bright ray of sunlight breaking through threatening clouds, Jesus stepped on the scene and immediately became a target of their hate.

The reason the world hated him so was that his light exposed their evil. It showed what they really were, and eventually led to the scene in Gethsemane.

Because of what Christ endured, our path may be illuminated so we may see the pitfalls of life. As a child of his, we have a guide through life. We do not have to travel this path by ourselves. He gives us something greater than ourselves to follow. It is a path of life and love, not one of death and hate.

And even though we may not fully understand all that is happening around us, he enlightens our mind and tells us we can trust his path. He only wants what is best for his children.

The next benefit we see from the oil is

Oil for medicine—a healing stream

His heart was *crushed*, so that our hearts might be mended.

This is expressed so eloquently in Isaiah 53:5 (KJV), **"But he was wounded for our transgressions, he was bruised for our iniquities: the chastisement of our peace was upon him; and with his stripes we are healed."**

There is a story told about a man named Tommy Dorsey. Thomas A. Dorsey was a jazz musician known as "Georgia Tom." He frequented jazz clubs and was a vaudeville star.

In 1921, at the age of twenty-two, he gave his heart to Jesus, left the jazz clubs, and began writing gospel music. Many have since dubbed him the "Father of Gospel Music."

One night while he was away from his pregnant wife's bedside performing at a revival meeting, his wife passed away, losing the child in the process.

For a while he struggled with the grief. He began to question why God would allow something like that to happen. He related that he doubted he could ever perform anything but secular music again. He would go back to the jazz clubs.

One evening, while with friends, he began to play on the piano. A melody began forming in his head and he started to play what he was hearing in his mind. From deep in his soul, words began flooding out.

Precious Lord, take my hand, lead me on, let me stand.
I am tired. I am weak. I am worn.
Through the storm, through the night, lead me on
to the light.
Take my hand, Precious Lord. Lead me home.

As this song poured out of him, the Lord started a healing process in his heart that was nothing short of miraculous. He experienced a supernatural peace that emanated from the throne room of heaven. That gospel song he wrote while in the depths of grief became a popular and very moving hymn that has touched the lives of millions.

Everyone who has ever lived has experienced, at one time or another, periods of hurt and pain. Their hearts or their minds have been wounded, and they may feel like there is no one who can truly understand what they are going through.

We have a savior who understands and sympathizes with us perfectly. He has walked that path before us. He has been in Gethsemane. He has suffered grief beyond anything we could ever imagine.

He is the one who can miraculously start a healing process in your heart. He applies the oil of his Spirit to the wounds in our hearts and minds. Whereas I may not know how to help, HE is all-knowing and all-loving. He can do what human ingenuity could never do.

The final benefit we will look at here is

Oil used in soap—cleansing

The past can be a very haunting memory. It can raise its head at the most inopportune moments, bringing with it a sense of shame and guilt.

Most people who have thrown away all caution and given into all sorts of sinful passions understand the feeling of "dirtiness" that can accompany this. Even a man who has tried to do right most of his life can, in an unguarded moment, slip into a sin that he never would have believed himself capable of.

That moment of indiscretion can "dog" a man the rest of his life. Some people never can manage to forgive themselves, and that feeling of "filth" hangs onto them like a worn-out shirt.

There is a wonderful promise given to us in 1 John 1:9 (KJV), **"If we confess our sins, he is faithful and just to forgive us our sins, and to cleanse us from all unrighteousness."**

That sinless man praying in Gethsemane is in the cleansing business. Not only does he forgive that sin, but he washes up the sinner. In its place, he leaves someone who is as clean as if he had never sinned in the first place.

Oh, the joy of having that "clean" sensation! The past might still be there, but praise God, there is no need to feel that guilt again. It has all been washed away.

* * * * *

Now that we have seen the *place* where it all happened, our attention is drawn to the *person* kneeling in that garden. This is the central figure in this tale.

Jesus Christ: Who was he?

CHAPTER 2

The Mystery of His Nature

We were surprised and a little bit flabbergasted. We had not expected to hear what we had just heard from our tour guide.

Our guide was a Palestinian man. I don't remember what his name was (it was forty-three years ago after all), but we called him Popo. The reason we called him that was because every time he wanted us to hurry up, he would say, "Popo. Shake a leg." I have no idea what that word meant, but from then on out, we called him Popo.

We had grown to expect him to cast doubt on our faith. He was of the Islamic belief. This was back in 1973, and Muslims were not constantly in the news as they are today. We had a very limited understanding of the Islamic religion.

We could remember standing at the ruins of Jericho and hearing him speak of the archaeology of the area and asserting that there was no way the city could have fallen the way the Bible said it did. More than once, what he said did not sit well with the Baptist preachers in our group.

He also didn't understand what all that we were seeing meant to us. While standing at the spot in the Jordan River where tradition said Jesus was baptized, many of the preachers wanted to be baptized in the Jordan like Jesus was. We had such a glorious time singing "Shall We Gather at the River," walking down into the Jordan, and being baptized. Popo's reaction was, "You came all the way out here to do that?"

So what he said took us by surprise.

We had left Gethsemane and had moved higher up the Mount of Olives to its very top. There was no doubt that right in this area was where Jesus left his disciples and had ascended back to heaven.

There are three sites that lay claim to being the specific spot where Jesus ascended. No one knows for sure where the exact spot was, or in fact, which of the three peaks of Olivet he left from. We were standing at one of the spots of tradition.

Popo was speaking relating the Bible story we knew so well, "While he was speaking to the disciples, he began to ascend back to heaven." Popo began to get excited.

"The disciples watched until a cloud received him from their sight." His level of excitement rose with each statement he made.

And then in a voice that almost sounded like an evangelical preacher, he said, "And THIS SAME JESUS who went away SHALL COME BACK AGAIN just as he left."

We were puzzled to say the least. We knew that Popo wasn't a Christian, so his declaration of Christ's return seemed out of character.

One of the preachers with us began to talk with him about that, "Do you believe that Jesus is coming back again?"

"Oh yes, Jesus will return."

"What do you believe about Jesus?"

"Jesus was a prophet but not the Son of God. He was just another man." He then launched into the standard mantra of faith in the Islamic religion.

So, in Popo's mind, there was nothing special or unique about this man named Jesus. This leads me to certain conclusions about Popo.

He got "excited" about Jesus.

He even believed he would return.

But...

What he believed *about* Jesus was wrong.

He didn't know who Jesus was.

* * * * *

There was nothing ordinary about this man Jesus. The whole crux of Christianity revolves around the person of Christ. If, indeed as I believe, he is who he claimed to be, then he cannot be treated as flippantly as people treat him. He, in fact, becomes the central figure of all mankind.

Jesus Christ, in fact, was 100% God, while at the same time 100% man. I think we make a mistake if we say he was "part" God and "part" man, but he was "fully" God and "fully" man. This is the mystery of his nature.

Before I launch into a discussion about him, let me admit something. I do not *understand* everything about God. I accept a lot of things by faith. But I'm *glad* I don't understand everything about him. If I could understand everything there was about God, he would be as *small* as my mind. Thank God, he transcends all that my mind could comprehend. He is a *big* God, who is able to meet any need I have far above any capacity of my own.

But there are some things that we can say with assurance about him, because they are spelled out in the scripture. Just one such example is found in the book of Hebrews.

God who at sundry times and in divers manners spake in time past unto the fathers by the prophets, Hath in these last days spoken unto us by *his* Son, whom he hath appointed heir of all things, by whom also he made the worlds; who being the brightness of his glory, and the express image of his person, and upholding all things by the word of his power, when he had by himself purged our sins, sat down on the right hand of the majesty on high; being made so much better than the angels, as he hath by

inheritance obtained a more excellent name than they. (Heb. 1:1–4, KJV)

This passage begins by asserting that Jesus Christ was *himself* the conclusive revelation of God. The Old Testament prophets revealed line upon line, just a piece at a time, as God's Spirit revealed it unto them. This revelation would culminate when the Word became flesh (John 1:1–14). I liken it to many small streams merging together into a mighty river that explodes into Niagara Falls.

Christ is the highpoint, the Mount Everest, of God's revelation to man.

The writer of the book of Hebrews then spreads before our eyes seven descriptive characteristics of the man Jesus. He begins with

He is the heir of all things

The Father appointed the Son to be "heir" of everything. There was no vote taken; no committee to decide. Mankind was not consulted. God in his infinite power has the right and made this determination.

This means that he is the rightful owner of everything that we see. All that I possess was given unto me for my use. I can freely partake of all the blessings that he has sent my way. I only need to realize that I have been given the responsibility to use it wisely.

Not only is he heir of all these "things," but by right, all that I am belongs to him. My very "self," my "being," or my soul should be available for his use. That is why refusal to acknowledge or give myself to him is such a grievous sin.

In spite of the fact that he has the right to me, He gives me a free will to choose to follow him or to reject him.

By his nature, he is heir of all things.

The next characteristic of the Son is

He created all we see

This man called Jesus, the one born in Bethlehem, was actually the Creator of the universe. Remember, the passage in Hebrews was speaking specifically about the Son. So, we can say with assurance that the one kneeling in the Garden of Gethsemane, talking to his Father, was the one who spoke the worlds into existence.

Jesus did not have his "beginning" in Bethlehem, but was everlasting to everlasting in eternity. That is just "preacher talk" for saying that he is infinite and has no beginning. As the second part of the Godhead, he was involved in Creation.

Bethlehem was merely his physical entrance onto the human stage.

If he formed all things, then *he actually formed you.* Having formed me, he knows exactly what I am like. He knows my personality with all of its quirks and peculiarities. He knows exactly what is best for me. Since he does, no one else is qualified to be our Lord.

This adds a new light to Gethsemane. While he is praying, I believe his infinite knowledge could foresee us individually. We will get into the ramifications of that later in the book, but for now, suffice it to say that this is mind-boggling.

The description of him does not end there.

He is the brightness of his glory

In Gethsemane, bowed beneath a load of grief, was the light of the world. Experiencing a period of personal darkness himself, he was the one who was to enlighten us and free us from *our* darkness.

The light first comes to expose man as he is. It exposes our sinful nature, revealing to us how truly horrendous our transgression of God's law is. This is why the world rails against the Cross so. They want to go on in their wickedness and not be bothered by the thought of a coming judgment.

In contrast, it shines the light upon Christ himself, and all we see is beauty. All God's glory, all his love, and all his majesty are wrapped up in this individual. What a picture it is! Everything pure, everything holy, and all the mercy that the world so desperately needs are on display for us to see.

There would seem to be no end to the accolades we could heap on him, but for the moment we must move on.

He is the express image of God

We are finite beings. We have a limited view of things. How could a person like myself ever understand such an exalted and majestic being as God?

Wrapped up in this man named Jesus was the perfect expression of the heart of God. We see walking along the shores of Galilee the compassion of the Father. We see, as Jesus calms the storm, the power of God on full display. We see God's power over death as Jesus calls out, "Lazarus, come forth!"

We can also see by the agony that Christ experienced in Gethsemane that God's heart can be broken. The waywardness of those he created squeezes his heart to the point of tears. And when he sees one of his in pain or distress, it moves his heart like nothing else could.

And because God came and walked among us, no one can point an accusing finger at God and say, "You don't understand. You don't know what it was like. It wasn't 'fair' what I went through."

He knows perfectly well what we experience in our everyday life. He has been there. Not only can he empathize with us, but he has conquered all that we face and demonstrates that there is a way of escape in every situation.

Jesus was God's expression to man.

Another characteristic we see in Jesus is his omnipotence.

He upholds all things by the Word of his power

Please remember, once again, that the one the author of the book of Hebrews is talking about is the *Son*. It is not some generic deity. It is very specific on whom it is speaking about. It is the Son of God; Jesus of Nazareth.

He upholds all things. Who keeps the worlds from colliding together? It is the Son. Who holds this universe in the palm of his hand? It is the Son. Who bears the weight of the world on his shoulders? It is the Son.

This intricate organism we call the human body was designed and woven together by his will; the word of his power.

Acts 17:28 (KJV) states, **"In him we live, and move, and have our being."** He holds our very breath and substance in his hands. Our life is balanced by much firmer hands than mine. This is why we can trust him.

I think of the atheist or the agnostic who rails against God and refuses to allow his rule over their lives. They never realize that their very life is in his hand, and it is only the long-suffering mercy of God that doesn't strike them down.

It is the love that Christ has for his Creation that stays his wrath. We will see this love played out in Gethsemane.

What the book of Hebrews next describes is the work that he does.

He made purification for our sins

One of the common denominators in all humans is the existence of sin. It is usually the hardest thing to convince people of. When the Holy Spirit, however, convicts or convinces a person that they are a sinner. It opens the door to a life-changing experience. Through the blood of Jesus, there is the cleansing and forgiveness of sin.

The blood of Jesus doesn't just "cover" our sin like Old Testament sacrifices did. It washes and *takes it away*, leaving us clean and pure.

There is no sin so dirty that the sinner cannot be made clean. It is absolutely true that **the blood of Jesus Christ his son cleanseth us from all sin** (1 John 1:7).

Finally, we can see what his position is now.

He sat down on the right hand of majesty

The one who was kneeling is now seated. Once praying to his Father, now he is exalted to this prominent position.

Once the atoning work was finished, He ascended to take his place by the throne. It was an enthronement worthy of royalty, and speaks of his deity. The supreme nature of his position demonstrates the honor, authority, and power that are rightfully his.

Perhaps the simplest thing we could say about his enthronement is that *he is worthy of our worship*. All praise and glory should be offered to him. It is rightfully his.

Daniel 7:13–14 (KJV) speaks of his enthronement:

> **I saw in the night visions, and, behold, one like the Son of man came with the clouds of heaven, and came to the Ancient of days, and they brought him near before him. And there was given to him dominion, and glory, and a kingdom, that all peoples, nations, and languages should serve him: his dominion is an everlasting dominion, which shall not pass away, and his kingdom that which shall not be destroyed.**

It is clear when we examine the central figure in the Gethsemane narrative that he was not an ordinary man. He was unique in every way.

Is there a mystery involved in his nature? Yes, but it is not one that should puzzle us. It is one we should embrace and rejoice in. We have such a wondrously lovely and complex savior who, because of his nature, can satisfy every need that we have.

On one hand, we have a unique man, unlike any who have ever walked before. On the other, we have a place of destiny, where opposing forces meet. It seems like an appropriate place for the clash to occur.

Let's use our imagination now and try to place ourselves in that garden on that night.

Step with me into the Garden of Gethsemane.

CHAPTER 3

The Mystery of His Prayer

What would this night have in store for them?

An uneasiness had crept over John's heart as they descended the path to the Kidron opposite the Mount of Olives. Earlier, as they had sat at supper with the Lord, there had been a sense of peace. It's true that Jesus had said some things that were troubling, but there was just something about being in his presence that made everything all right.

Now, as they were approaching Gethsemane, the night had taken on an ominous mood. Even the atmosphere seemed to utter a warning of what lay ahead.

John began to reflect on some of the things that had taken place the past couple of days. Confusion doesn't begin to describe how the men in this little band felt. There had been the reluctance to depart for Jerusalem for fear of what might happen. This was followed by being suddenly swept up in joy as the crowds closer to Jerusalem began to cry out, "Hosanna! Hosanna to the son of David! Blessed is he that comes in the name of the Lord!"

Just as quickly that joy had dissipated as Jesus topped the Mount of Olives to gaze upon the city of Jerusalem. He began to cry and lament the fate of the city.

There were so many things that had happened in a short period of time that it was beginning to seem like a blur.

Perhaps when it really began to take shape in John's mind was a few days previously, while they had been at supper in Simon's house. Simon had been healed of leprosy by the Lord and Jesus had been invited along with the disciples, Mary, and Martha to a supper.

In the middle of supper, Mary had approached the Master, knelt beside him, and opened up a bottle of perfume. The fragrance filled the room. There was no mistaking it. It was myrrh; extremely expensive.

She poured a little on his feet and then a little on his head. John could see from where he was that she was crying. With nothing to wipe his feet with, she loosened her long hair and began to use it to wipe his feet.

The indignation began with Judas. He turned to one of the other disciples and whispered in a low voice, "What a waste! Do you know how many people we could have fed with the price of myrrh? Surely the poor are more important than anointing someone's feet."

That seemed logical and before long, he had the entire group muttering to themselves.

The Lord turned his attention to his disciples. It always seemed like he knew what they were thinking. "Why do you question what Mary has done? Leave her alone. She has done a good work to me. You will always have opportunity to help the poor."

He then spoke the words that were haunting John, "She has done this to prepare me for my *burial*."

For my burial, were the words that were sticking out in John's mind.

There had been so many times recently when Jesus spoke of dying. Maybe that was what attributed to John's rising apprehension about this night.

They continued on the path till they reached the foot of the Mount of Olives. There was Gethsemane. They had resorted here before, and it had always seemed like a quiet and peaceful place to pray. Tonight, however, there seemed to be something very unsettling awaiting them. John couldn't quite put his finger on it, but it was almost as if a sinister presence was beckoning to them.

Entering the garden, John noticed for the first time that, in the dark, the twisted trunks of the olive trees resembled frightening figures with long arms reaching out to embrace them. It was almost like a childhood dream where unseen monsters awaited you.

Perhaps even more troubling to John was the obvious look of distress that had enveloped the Master. In every situation, he had always been so calm and in control. Whether it was a storm on the sea or the opposition of the Pharisees, nothing ever seemed to faze him.

Tonight, he appeared as he had never seen him before.

Jesus turned to his disciples and said, "If there ever was a time for prayer, it is now. Peter, James, John; come with me. The rest of you please wait here."

They went a little farther and came to the olive press. Jesus turned to the three disciples and said, "Wait here and pray. What I deal with tonight I must face alone, but stay here. Watch and pray."

John watched as Jesus proceeded on alone. He knelt by a large rock and John could tell he was beginning to converse with his Father.

The Lord had asked them to pray, but John didn't know what to pray for.

As the time passed, he noticed that Peter and James had begun to nod off to sleep. The past few days had been emotionally draining, and this day had already been long.

Slowly, John began to drift off to sleep.

* * * * *

Prayer was an indispensable part of the life of Jesus. The scripture often refers to the fact that Jesus went aside, alone, to pray. Every step he took was literally bathed in prayer.

Some of his prayers are recorded for us to see. The most well-known is what is referred to as the Lord's Prayer. How often we have felt a sense of comfort by repeating the Lord's Prayer. But in reality, it is the model prayer. It describes to us how we are to pattern our own prayers.

Jesus's high priestly prayer is recorded in John 17. In it, we see the majesty of prayer. Jesus prays for his disciples, and by extension, prays for us. It is truly an amazing prayer.

Another prayer that sticks out in my mind is right before the feeding of the five thousand, when he blessed and multiplied the loaves and fishes. Although the words are not recorded, it must have been some kind of blessing.

Of all the prayers he prayed, I don't think any have had the impact on my life like the prayer in Gethsemane. It is noted for its brevity; only two recorded sentences. The implications of this brief petition can truly be life altering. There is no way to soften the impact of those words.

It is made up of two parts: an opening and a closing. The opening of the prayer is **"Father, if it be possible, let this cup pass from me."** The closing is, **"Nevertheless, not my will but thine be done."**

It is the opening of the prayer that poses a mystery to me. I wonder why the Lord prayed this. What was transpiring at that time that caused him to pray in this manner?

The mystery of his words, I believe, are intertwined with the mystery of his nature. As we explored in the previous chapter, Jesus was fully *God*, yet at the same time, fully *man*. The only way to fully appreciate his words are in that light.

Let's examine this mystery a little more closely.

The cross did not catch Jesus by surprise

Jesus knew full well that he had come into this world to die, and foretold it many times. One day, while Jesus was with his disciples in the town of Caesarea Philippi, he began to question his disciples.

"Who do men say that I am?" he asked.

They replied, "Some people say that you are John the Baptist come back from the dead. Other people say that you are Elijah, or one of the other prophets."

"But who do you say that I am?" he pressed.

Peter took the lead. "Thou art the Christ foretold in scripture."

At this Jesus began to foretell of his passion as recorded in Mark 8:31 (KJV):

And he began to teach them that the Son of Man must suffer many things, and be rejected of the elders, and of the chief priests, and scribes, and be *killed*, and after three days rise again.

He was so plain in his teaching that Peter, who had just made such a great statement of faith, took him aside and began to disagree with him saying, "This isn't going to happen."

Peter contended with him so strongly that the Lord had to rebuke him in the strongest terms possible.

Throughout his ministry, the shadow of the Cross loomed over Jesus. Every step he took directed him toward an appointment in Jerusalem. Every time Jesus tried to bring up the subject and prepare his disciples, they did not want to hear it.

As he moved closer and closer to Jerusalem, his fame preceded him. Crowds would gather along the way. With the many miracles he did, there was quite a stir and a great crowd approaching Jerusalem.

The commotion that preceded his triumphal entry into Jerusalem drew the focus of the entire city to Jesus. While the Pharisees were busy conspiring against him, there were others of Greek descent who were earnestly desiring to see Jesus. It seems like there was a sharp divide in the way people viewed him. Some sought to see if this was indeed the Anointed One, while others were of the judgment that he was a threat to their standing.

It was in this setting that Jesus began to speak, as recorded in John 12, in a way that foreshadowed what was about to occur.

"The hour has arrived," he began, "when the Son of Man shall be glorified." He then began to speak using the illustration of wheat being sown in the ground, dying, and bringing forth fruit.

To the disciples much of what he was saying probably sounded like things they had heard before. The meaning of it was probably lost on them for he was speaking of loving your life and losing it. He went on to "If any man serve me, let him follow me." This was all so familiar and was similar to what they had already heard.

But then, something changed in the way Jesus was speaking. His visage was altered, showing distress. He then said some things that previewed what he would pray in the Garden. The similarities are undeniable.

> **Now is my soul troubled; and what shall I say? Father, save me from this hour: but for this cause came I unto this hour.** (Jn 12:27, KJV)

There it is sitting right in front of us. The foreshadowing of his prayer. It could not have escaped the disciples attention, for the Father spoke from heaven in their presence glorifying and verifying that this was his Son.

This passage tells us two things about Jesus at this point in time. *Jesus knew what was about to happen to him.* There was nothing hid from him. He was proceeding down that path knowing full well what awaited him.

The second thing that is evident is that Jesus knew that *this was his purpose; the reason he came into this world.* This unique person who was 100% God and 100% man was fully aware of what approached.

It is almost as if Jesus is asking himself if this is the way he *should* pray.

This is the mystery that is wrapped up in the words he would pray in Gethsemane. "Father, if it be possible, let this cup pass from me."

There is something else we must consider while we reflect on his prayer.

His hand was not forced

Jesus was not backed into a corner. There was no external force making him go to the cross.

Simply put, Jesus did not have to redeem us. He would have been perfectly justified to just leave us in our sin. After all, we were the ones that rebelled against God. It was not God who had wronged us. It was mankind, that walked away from and disrupted our relationship with God.

Who was there that was powerful enough to make God do anything? There was no power or force that could stand up to Almighty God. If indeed there were, as I believe, sinister demonic beings arrayed around the Lord as he prayed in Gethsemane, sent to torment him, their power paled when compared to the one kneeling there.

There was something else, within the Lord himself, that propelled him to the cross. We will examine that more closely in a following chapter.

The proof of the fact that no one forced him to his fate is found in the ways he *did not* defend himself.

The unused defenses

The first defense that Jesus refused to use was *armed self-defense.* When the temple guard came into the garden, led by Judas, there was one meager attempt by Peter to defend the Lord. He drew a dagger and swung it at one of the guards named Malchus. While Peter was swinging for his head, he only managed to slice a part of his ear.

No doubt, while their attention was temporarily turned to armed Peter, Jesus performed an amazing act of mercy by reaching out and healing the ear of one of the men sent to arrest him. Could you imagine how Malchus probably felt looking into the eyes of Jesus. The Lord was literally living out his teaching to "do good to those who hate you."

Turning to Peter, he then began to chide him, "Put up your dagger. Those who live by the sword will surely die by the sword." With those words the disciples began to turn and flee the area.

Jesus had at his disposal eleven men who could have surrounded him. Instead of crying out, "Defend yourselves!" he, in effect, told them, "This is not the way I taught you."

Even though they were arresting him illegally, he refused to call upon his disciples to protect him.

The second defense he refused to use was *soaring rhetoric*. During his entire trial, both before Caiaphas and Pilate, Jesus refused to put up a defense.

One of the things that was said about Jesus was that "no one spoke like this man." By the power of his words, he could hold multitudes spellbound. No one would have been better qualified to lay out his defense than Jesus himself. Yet, he did not defend his actions, nor challenge the falsehoods brought against him.

It brings to mind the prophecy in the book of Isaiah:

> **He was oppressed, and he was afflicted, yet he opened not his mouth: he is brought as a lamb to the slaughter, and as a sheep before his shearers is dumb, so he openeth not his mouth.** (Is. 53:7, KJV)

The third defense he refused to use was *His Father's intervention*. After he had rejected Peter's feeble attempt at an armed defense, Jesus interjected this, "Do you not know that even now I could call on my Father to protect me? He would send twelve legions of angels to defend me."

At his disposal were unseen spiritual armies; waiting on a word from him. All he would have had to do was say the word and they would have swarmed around him. No one could have touched him. They, in fact, had the firepower to destroy all who made a threatening move against the Lord.

Of all the defenses he could have relied upon, this one was the most potent. Jesus refused to avail himself of it. He would not this ask of his Father.

This proves beyond a doubt that Jesus wasn't forced against his will to the cross. In fact, it shows where his heart was.

He would not make an armed defense.

He would not use soaring rhetoric.

He would not ask his Father to intervene.

He was willingly allowing himself to be taken. He was not blindsided but submitted to it with his eyes wide open. This adds to the mystery surrounding the words that he prayed.

What was there about what was happening in Gethsemane that prompted him to open the prayer as he did?

CHAPTER 4

What Prompted the Opening of His Prayer?

John awoke with a start. Peter had been nudging him saying, "It's the master."

The usual grogginess one feels when coming out of a deep sleep seemed to evaporate immediately. Perhaps this was due to an uneasy sense that something was going on.

There Jesus stood before them. "What? Could you not watch with me for only an hour?"

The feeling of apprehension that John had felt previously intensified with just one look at the Lord. It was almost as if his visage had changed. He had never seen Jesus quite like this. His haggard look made it appear as if he had been in a wrestling match. He certainly had been struggling with something. John thought he detected a pain and weariness in his eyes that he had never detected before.

"Watch and pray, that you enter not into temptation."

With those words, a feeling of guilt washed over John. At such a dire time, how could he have drifted off to sleep?

John looked over at Peter and James and realized that they had been asleep too.

John took a closer look at Jesus and was shocked by what he saw. There appeared to be blood running down his forehead, seemingly coming out of his very pores. A shiver suddenly ran down his spine. There was that sense again, that something evil was lurking nearby.

He couldn't quite put his finger on it, but it was evident to John that something was going on. Unlike Jesus, who always seemed to know beforehand what was happening, John was often caught by surprise by events. He wasn't all that sure he wanted to face something like that tonight. Was something terrifying about to happen?

John watched as Jesus turned to go back to his personal communion with the Father.

Once again, he felt a helplessness in knowing what to pray for. That feeling of not knowing how to put what he was feeling into words made praying one of the most frustrating exercises he had ever attempted.

What was about to happen?

How could he pray?

John watched as Jesus began to kneel continuing his prayer.

What was Jesus saying in his prayer?

* * * * *

"Father, if it be possible, let this cup pass from me."

It is always hard to place yourself in someone else's shoes and try to imagine what is going on in their lives. Try as I might, I can never seem to fully appreciate all that the other person is enduring. That is because I bring my own experiences and insight into the mix. I have walked a different path than that other person has walked.

So, it is an admittedly dauntless task to try and imagine *all* that the Savior experienced in the garden. The enormity of it would far outstrip my mind to comprehend it. That is why I don't think we could ever fully understand his agony. In fact, I doubt that we could handle it, even if we could see it.

Understanding that it is certainly an incomplete viewing of what Christ experienced in Gethsemane, I would like to offer some suggestions to perhaps get a glimpse of what was happening that night.

What prompted the opening of his prayer?

There are five things that I believe were weighing upon our Savior that night.

His mortal pain

I do not think we can discount the horror that the physical pain of crucifixion evoked in people. I really don't want to get into the gory details of it, but an examination of the nature of crucifixion might illuminate our minds to what the thought would produce in an individual.

Crucifixion was a *political tool* that the Romans used in an effort to quell insurgencies. It was basically a show of power intended to ward off or warn future insurgents. If the actions of a state can be termed terrorism by the fear it produced in a populace, then crucifixion could be termed a "state act of terror." It was designed to produce fear.

It was extremely effective. The reason it was effective was that it was a particularly cruel form of torture. Its goal was not merely to execute, but to inflict as much pain as possible. At this the Romans excelled. For a society that prided itself as being the most civilized in the world, it could be the most barbaric.

It was a *lingering death*. The length of time it took could depend on several factors. The physical shape that the person was in, or his treatment beforehand could shorten or lengthen the experience. Beating or scourging prior to crucifixion would serve to weaken the individual. In that sense, the six hours it took for Jesus to die was a comparatively short time, for many languished upon a cross for days.

There were many possible causes of death through crucifixion. One such cause was *exhaustive asphyxia*. To be able to breathe properly, the malefactor would have to push up on his feet, taking the pressure off of his hands. After a while, exhaustion would set in and the person would settle down and slowly suffocate.

Another possibility was *pulmonary edema* where you had a buildup of pressure around the heart. This would result in heart failure. The clear fluid that would collect in the lungs might explain the blood and water that flowed from Jesus's side.

There is a whole list of other potential causes of death. Heart rupture, hypoglycemic shock, heart arrhythmias, dehydration, exposure, or heart clots in the lungs. Not being a doctor, this list might seem overwhelming, but the end result was the same: a slow death.

The point of it all was to inflict pain and make it last as long as possible. That is what made crucifixion a thing to be feared.

But I believe there were some things far more apprehensive that was weighing on the heart of Jesus than mere physical pain.

The loneliness of its shame

The very thought of the cross brought a loneliness to the heart of Christ. He never made a move toward it without finding himself alone. Peter himself, as we have previously mentioned, chided the Lord when he spoke of his death. There are so many places in scripture where he foretold his death and his resurrection. Every time he did, it was as if the disciples would try to push it out of their minds, and Jesus would find himself standing alone.

It was as if the disciples were caught by surprise when the Lord was arrested and led away. It seems somehow unbelievable that the disciples would not have grasped this truth. Yet, somehow, they would not allow their minds to wrap around this idea. It was so foreign to their expectations.

When Jesus finally arrives in the garden, he finds that the disciples cannot even stay awake long enough to pray with him during this time of trial. He was alone again.

There are different types of loneliness. There is the *loneliness of solitude*. Jesus often resorted alone to pray. This kind of solitude can be a very constructive thing. To separate oneself in order to clear one's mind, pray, and take on a different perspective can be very positive. Jesus was well acquainted with doing this.

There is also the *loneliness of character*, where a person may be in a crowd and still feel alone. In one place, when someone promised to follow him, Jesus had responded:

The foxes have holes, and the birds of the air have nests; but the Son of Man hath not where to lay his head. (Matt. 8:20, KJV)

The Lord had accepted this kind of loneliness. He knew that his followers would have a difficult time understanding what his true mission in this world was. As much as he tried to explain it, they had a difficult time grasping it.

I believe that what was weighing upon Jesus in Gethsemane was what I call the *loneliness of its shame*. Let me explain if I may.

In a few hours, the Father would turn his back on the Son. When Jesus cried out from the cross, "My God! My God! Why hast thou forsaken me?" it was not a mistaken notion.

Some have tried to suggest that it must have just "seemed" like he had been forsaken, and that he was merely quoting scripture. Because it strikes at their sensibilities, they seem to suggest that this turning of the Father away from the Son never took place. This would suggest that Jesus was mistaken, that he was wrong about something. To say that Jesus made a mistake would make him less than who he is. We've already covered his unique nature. It would mean that God is not all-knowing.

Those who suggest this miss the entire point. Jesus was dying in *our place*. It was a substitutional death. He was suffering what we deserved to suffer.

Because *we deserved to be forsaken,* he took our place and was forsaken for us. Therefore, we would not have to be forsaken, but could have a relationship with God.

What Jesus was about to face was very real. No man can fully understand the intimacy between the Father and Jesus. The schism that would temporarily separate the two would have weighed heavily upon the Lord. Is it any wonder that the anguish Jesus suffered in Gethsemane was so acute?

Along with this separation, there would have been a level of shame experienced. Let me reiterate, it was not his own shame, but he was bearing OUR shame.

It is hard for us to even comprehend the loneliness that flooded over the Savior as he prayed in the garden. The loneliness of its shame must have felt devastating.

His mental anguish

Jesus made the statement in the garden that he was exceedingly sorrowful "even unto death." Although it is not quite clear exactly what Jesus intended with this phrase, we do know something about death itself. Death passed upon all mankind because of sin. Jesus was sinless in his nature. As the God-Man, the sentence of death was not upon him. The idea of death was so foreign to his nature. To willingly face something like death for others when he did not have to must have weighed heavily upon his mind.

We make a mistake if we think that God's will is always easy. Sometimes it is extremely difficult. What Jesus was about to face was difficult beyond belief.

Whenever God marks a path for us that is not easy, we need to remind ourselves that *God's will is good*. It is good for what it produces *in* us and what it produces *for* us.

Although it would produce great things for us, there is no question that it was the most difficult thing that Jesus had ever done.

There is no way to imagine what his mental anguish would have been like.

The desolation of his soul

This would have affected more than just his mind. It would strike at his very soul. To any person, the soul would seem desolated when it sensed that God was no longer near.

This separation is usually caused by sin. That's why when a Christian commits sin, there is an immediate sense of despair and Holy Spirit conviction that floods his soul.

But Jesus had no sin to despair about. He was the sinless, spotless Lamb of God. There never was a soul purer and holier than his. He walked this earth, yet was untainted and unpolluted by its evil. Then why the desolation?

There was something momentous taking place at this time.

Upon Christ, a sinless soul, was being placed the sin of the *entire world.*

I know. I can almost hear the objections. There is a hyper-Calvinistic line of thought that insists that since only the elect will be saved, that Jesus did not die for the sins of the entire world. He only died for the sins of the elect.

The only problem with that reasoning is that it does not match itself up very well with scripture. For our purposes here, I will share just one instance of this out of the book of 1 Timothy.

The Apostle Paul, in the second chapter, instructs us to pray for all men, including our leaders. He then concludes:

> **For this is good and acceptable in the sight of God our Savior; who will have _all_ men to be saved, and to come unto the knowledge of the truth. For there is one God, and one mediator between God and men, the man Christ Jesus who gave himself *a ransom for all* to be testified in due time. (1 Tim. 2:3–6, KJV)**

There it is stated plainly. Jesus was taking upon himself the sin of the entire world. *All* who would ever live, would have their sins placed upon this precious sacrifice.

Think of how heavy a weight that would be. What if the sins of every person who lives in your town were lumped together in one place and the responsibility for it was placed on one person. How great would that load be?

Expand it out now. Let's pull together all the sins of our state and then on to the entire country. Every sin committed today in the entire United States of America would really mount up. Factor in, then, every sin in the entire world. It becomes unimaginable. We will use the phrase "the sins of the entire world" and not really grasp the magnitude of it.

We can't stop here, however. Think not just of the sins of our day and age. Think of every sin since creation.

Can you see the heavy load that was being placed on Jesus? The significance of it is truly mind boggling. Can you see the love of the Lord portrayed here? Does your heart break, knowing that I contributed to that load?

Think with me now about the types of sin placed upon the Lord.

There are some sins that are so repugnant and disgusting that I don't even like to talk about them. I don't even like to think about them, and I will not name them here.

Consider the worst possible sin you could think of. The vilest, most repulsive sins imaginable were being placed on the pure and holy Son of God. This precious, spotless Lamb who had never known the taint of sin was now bearing the worst of the worst. Oh, how it breaks my heart in two to realize the level of what the Lord bore for us!

Can you begin to understand a little of the agony that was tearing at the Lord in Gethsemane?

The rejection of his love by so many

With all that was going on in Gethsemane, could it have been that knowing so many would reject his offer of salvation was breaking his heart? Here was the Lord suffering through all this pain for those he loved, and yet there are so many who will have nothing to do with it.

The most glaring example of this was Judas. He was one of the twelve. He didn't merely reject the Lord. In fact, he put on the façade of being a follower. This man who put on such a front went so far as to betray the Lord.

Could you imagine walking with the Lord for three years, enjoying the camaraderie of the twelve, yet being so evil hearted that he gave up the Lord for money? The suffering this caused Jesus must have been great. To an ordinary person like myself, it might have seemed like it was too much to bear.

But it was more than just Judas or the mob that cried out, "Crucify him!" There were untold millions who would refuse his offer of eternal life throughout the coming years. There would also be an innumerable host that, like Judas, would wear the façade of being a follower of Christ but would actually be wolves in sheep's clothing.

Although it is not stated in scripture, I have speculated that there may have been demonic forces present in the garden sent to torment Jesus. The very fact that angels appeared to minister to and strengthen the Lord might have been in response to this.

Could they have been whispering in his ear, "There is no use in going through this. Those people will not receive you. They will reject you. They will even oppose the speaking of your name in public. You are wasting your time."

* * * * *

This is just a small suggestion of what Jesus must have been dealing with as he knelt in Gethsemane. As I have stated before, I still don't think I can fully grasp the extent of his suffering.

Can you begin to get a picture of what the Lord went through for you and me?

But his opening sentence was not the last word. Thank God for the way he closed out his prayer.

CHAPTER 5

What Inspired the Closing of His Prayer?

The rustling sound in the distance was drawing closer with each second. It sounded like an approaching mob, but at this time of night? If they were trying to use stealth, they weren't being very successful.

John turned and noticed that Jesus had reappeared beside them. "It's time to get up," he intoned. "The betrayer is here."

Jesus had spoken earlier in the upper room that someone would betray him, and here he was mentioning it again. John just could not for the life of him wrap his mind around that one. He knew all these people personally. He just could not envision any of them turning on the Lord. He would trust any one of them with his own life.

As the horde came into view, John was trying to make out who was leading this little band. In the dark, it was hard to make out, but there was something vaguely familiar about the one in the lead. There was something about the way he walked and deported himself that made John think, "I should know this guy."

Slowly the realization dawned on him.

No! It can't be true! he thought. *Not Judas!*

It soon became evident as the group began to enter the garden area. The mob, all of them seemed armed, stayed back a step. It was Judas who walked boldly toward the Lord.

"Hail, Master!" he said with a forced bravado, as he embraced him and gave him a greeting on the cheek.

The Lord looked Judas straight in the eyes. The look spoke of disappointment more than that of being wounded. Judas could not hold his gaze, but backed away a step or two with bowed head.

"Judas, do you betray the Son of Man with a kiss?" Judas could give no answer.

Jesus then turned toward the mob. "Whom do you seek?"

"Jesus of Nazareth," they answered.

"I am he."

They were such simple words, but spoken with such authority that the group seemed to be taken aback. John really couldn't tell if it was the force of his words or the sudden lunge at them by Peter that caused them to backpedal. One tripped over a rock and fell causing a couple of others to go cascading after him.

Peter had drawn and swung his dagger at the nearest guard, striking him around the ear. With a loud scream the man fell to his knees, clutching the side of his head.

The nearest guards began to grapple with Peter for control of his dagger. Everyone's attention was turned toward the struggle. In the confusion of this fray, with half of the men trying to pick themselves up off of the ground, no one other than John seemed to notice what the Lord was doing.

He gently walked over and laid his hand on the ear of the guard. A look of utter amazement swept over the man's face as he looked up into the eyes of Jesus. There was no longer any look of pain in his eyes, but of surprise and wonder. He remained on his knees, seemingly unable to move from the spot.

Jesus then turned his attention to the struggle going on.

"Peter! Put up your dagger!" His voice cut through the darkness with much more power than Peter's knife ever could.

The wrestling seemed to pause in mid action.

"I told you I am he," he addressed the crowd. "Let these others go!"

There was that authority again; spoken with such conviction that all action ceased.

Sensing his opportunity, Peter spun out of their grip, and disappeared into the gathering gloom. It was if a bell had rung, as all of the disciples turned and scattered into the night. John found himself running right along behind them.

At some point, John stopped and looked behind them. The Lord had been shackled, and was being led out of Gethsemane. They were proceeding up the path over the Kidron and up Zion leading to the high priest's house.

Events had been set in motion.

There seemed to be no recourse left to them.

He watched as the Lord was led to his destiny.

* * * * *

By the time Jesus was arrested in the garden, the issue had already been settled in the heart of Jesus. What lay before him was a trial and the most unpleasant form of death devised by man. There would be no appeal in this court. The outcome was preordained, seemingly set in stone.

Let me reemphasize what I have previously stated. No one forced his hand. He did not have to redeem us!

In Gethsemane, standing at the crossroad of decision, our very salvation hung in the balance. Would Jesus follow the path marked by the Father? Would he call twelve legions of angels to deliver him?

Was there ever any doubt?

"Nevertheless, let not my will but thine be done."

With those words, Jesus eliminated any doubt as to the outcome. If words are indeed important and *what* you say carries weight, then these must be some of the most significant words ever spoken.

You can talk about all sorts of words that have altered history. You can talk about the Magna Carte, The Declaration of Independence, The Emancipation Proclamation, or the Gettysburg Address. All of them are some of the greatest words ever spoken which have impacted the course of history. Our world has become a better place because of them.

But these words spoken in the garden of Gethsemane impacted *eternity*. There will be an innumerable host whose eternal destination has been altered because of those words.

On a personal note, *my* life has been affected because of those words. The joy of the Lord that I can experience, the personal relationship I have with my Creator, and the eternal home that is mine have all been made possible because those words were spoken. If you know the Lord, you can say the same.

Oh, how blessed these words are! How they can stir the heart to realize the Lord's willingness to bear our sin for us!

What an example it is of how I should conduct my life. As a follower of Christ, what a difference it would make in my life if in everything I said, "Lord, not my will, but thine be done."

To sum it all up, every aspect of life in this world or the world to come has been enhanced because of what Jesus would accomplish in the next few hours.

I believe there were at least four factors that moved him to take the path he took.

Submission to the Father's will

By any narrative, the most prominent characteristic of Jesus's life was the fact that he was obedient to the Father's will. The sheer number of times in the Gospels that Jesus spoke of his Father's will attest to that fact. Every step he took was in submission to His Father.

The book of Philippians speaks of his submission:

> **Let this mind be in you, which was also in Christ Jesus; who, being in the form of God, thought it not robbery to be equal with God; but made himself of no reputation, and took upon him the form of a servant, and was made in the likeness of men; and being found in fashion as a man, He humbled himself, and**

**became obedient unto death, even the death
of the cross.**

**Wherefore God hath highly exalted him,
and given him a name which is above every
name: that at the name of Jesus every knee
should bow, of things in heaven, and things
in earth, and things under the earth; and
that every tongue should confess that Jesus
Christ is Lord, to the glory of God the Father.**
(Phil. 2:5–11, KJV).

Jesus said at one time, "I do always those things that please him
(the Father)." (Jn 8:29, KJV).

There seems to be an amazing unpretentiousness in the makeup
of the Trinity. This passage states that the Father has highly exalted
the Son. Hebrews says that he has given the Son preeminence. The
Holy Spirit, for his part, "speaks not of himself" but "glorifies the
Son." (John 16:13–14). In keeping with that same mindset, Jesus is
in total submission to the Father.

I don't know how to explain this or describe this, except to use
human terms. Do you call it the "humility" of the Godhead, where
they constantly shift the spotlight to another person in the Trinity?
Using human characteristics like that doesn't quite seem adequate
when describing a Holy God.

At any rate, the single greatest principle that guided the Lord as
he walked this earth was submission to the Father's will.

So when it came to Gethsemane, there would be no other
path to follow. This submission effectively settled the question and
removed any doubt about what course he would take.

He became obedient unto death.

In fact, the Father's will had been determined long before
Gethsemane. Revelation 13:8 (KJV) refers to him as the **"Lamb
slain from the foundation of the world."** When God spoke, "Let
there be light," he had determined that the Son would come to be the
light of the world. When he breathed into Adam the breath of life,

He knew that Jesus would be "the way, the truth, and *the life.*" When he formed the living creatures including the meek animal called a lamb, he had already designated our Lord as "the lamb of God."

So it was, when faced with the prospect of enduring the physical pain of crucifixion, Christ took the form of a servant and prayed, "Not my will but thine be done."

Jesus's submission guaranteed that he would travel the path that led to Golgotha. It settled the question.

Settled for all time.

Settled before time.

But I believe there were other factors that moved Jesus to close his prayer as he did.

His love for us

Throughout Jesus's entire walk on this earth, he loved the multitudes that gathered around him. At least ten times in the Gospels it is recorded that he was "moved with compassion." In some instances, this compassion was directed toward an individual. In other instances, he was moved toward the multitude in general. It was usually prompted when he saw their plight or condition.

In Matthew 9:36 (KJV), it says that his compassion stirred when he looked upon the multitude **"because they fainted, and were scattered abroad, as sheep having no shepherd."**

Luke 7 recounts the story of Jesus and his followers coming across a funeral procession in Nain. Looking upon the mother, a widow who was about to bury her only son, he had compassion on her. After some words of comfort to the mother, he touched the bier, spoke to the dead, and life entered into the young man. Once again it was his love for this woman that caused him to act.

In Mark 10, the scripture recounts the story of a rich man who came to Jesus asking, "What must I do to inherit eternal life?" Jesus asked him if he knew the law, and the man responded that he had kept it from is youth.

It is recorded that Jesus was moved by a love for this man, and responded. "There is one thing that you lack." He then singled out the one thing that he loved more than the Lord, his wealth. The man, not wishing to part with his wealth, left with his head down.

Here is an instance of Jesus loving someone who would reject him. Could you imagine how the Lord felt watching this man walk away, knowing what the consequences of rejecting him would be? The pain that Jesus must have felt would be the same that he feels today when someone rejects him.

Every action Jesus took, every word he spoke, and every healing touch from his hand was a great big *I love you* note sent to all those around him. The one thing that motivated him as he walked among us was LOVE.

It is really astounding when you realize who *the object of his love* was.

The crowds that followed Jesus were not exactly the crème of society. Someone who is unkind might have called them the "unwashed" throng. They were not the elite. They were not the ones you invited to a dinner party. Among them were the sick, the maimed, and the outcast; the dregs of society. If you had looked closely you would have found some that were classified as "fallen."

When I called them "unwashed" that could also be applied literally. Hygiene in that day is not what it is today. People did not take baths with the regularity that we do. Not to be indelicate, but when you got a crowd of them together, the collected body odor would have been overwhelming.

Their manner would often have been abrupt. When barter was your exchange system, as it often was, you developed the art of haggling. This developed an argumentative nature in many.

To sum it all up, they would have been called brutish. There was nothing lovely or "likable" about them.

Yet when Jesus looked at them, with all their faults, he was consumed by an overwhelming LOVE for them. He saw them as lost with no direction and it broke his heart. He could not withhold his hand of healing or of mercy from them.

He *did* love the unlovely.

I believe that when he knelt in Gethsemane those people that he had walked with flooded his mind. *Love would compel him* to go to a cross of Calvary. There was just too much love in him to do otherwise.

There was also something else driving him.

He had a holy vision

Human vision can only see so far. We cannot see the future. We don't know what might happen tomorrow. All an ordinary man could have seen was an approaching death.

It seemed like the end.

As we covered in chapter two, Jesus was not just an ordinary man.

I believe with all my heart, that in the Garden Jesus, being God, had a *holy vision that looked beyond the cross.* Whereas the human could look and see only death, the divine looked beyond and saw a resurrection morning.

While praying in such agony, the forces sent to torment the Savior were no doubt saying, "This is the last that the world will hear of Jesus. All your good work will amount to nothing. It will end today."

But that holy vision looked forward three days and saw only *GLORY!*

Past the pain, past the suffering, he could see life flooding the tomb. He saw himself stepping out into the brightness of a new morning conquering a foe that seemed unbeatable. He saw a world that instead of wallowing in hopelessness could experience the joy of exclaiming, "HE IS RISEN! JESUS LIVES!"

With his eyes focused on the joy, he would step through the dark door of death and the GLORY would explode in blossoms of life that all could partake in.

We can experience that same glory, that joy, in knowing that this world is not all there is. He has conquered death, and because he did, we can too.

But I believe that his holy vision went beyond that. I believe that he could look down through history and see *the thousands of lives that would be changed* because of what he would accomplish on the cross. He could see a new bride, the church, waiting at the altar of heaven for his entrance.

If I may make it a little personal, I believe he could see to the year 1964. There at an altar in the Chattahoochee Baptist Church, a boy ten years of age would kneel down and call upon his name. That boy named Jimmy (that's me) would have his life forever changed. From then on, the two of them, Jesus and Jimmy, would start a relationship that would grow through every step they walked together.

If you have experienced that life-altering spiritual birth, you can think back to the day Jesus came into your life. I believe with all my heart that as he prayed in the Garden, JESUS SAW YOU!

I'm so thankful that Jesus had a holy vision that looked beyond the cross and saw us. He gladly bore the grief so that we could be reclaimed.

He would die so that others might live.

But there was something else that moved the Lord.

Faith

Jesus's entire life was marked by a confidence. It was a confidence born out of a faith in the Father's *character*. Because of his intimate connection to the Father, he knew the Father's heart. His faith was that the Father's desire for his creation would come to pass.

It was a faith in the Father's *ability* to accomplish his design and bring it to pass. He could see the finished product of salvation, and knew that by following the Father's will, it would be accomplished.

You've heard it said that actions speak louder than words; a demonstration is more convincing than a declaration. So, when Jesus was in the Garden of Gethsemane, he became a living demonstration to his disciples of something he had been trying to teach them. *Live your life by faith.*

When you are faced with a heartbreaking situation, Jesus's example teaches us to trust that God is still in control. We can trust that the Father will work his will out in our lives. Just as you trusted him for your salvation, you are to trust him for every aspect of your life.

To tie it all up, in Gethsemane Jesus recognized that the cup was given to him by the Father. His confidence in the Father caused him to follow the path to Golgotha.

* * * * *

Along with the sins of the world, the worst agonies that the world could ever prescribe were heaped upon the Son of God. From the most horrible terrors in the night to the torment inflicted by demonic forces, they were all experienced by Jesus that night. Gethsemane was the place where we begin to see just what our sin would cost the Lord.

Because of his matchless love for us, he would walk that road, but the pressures of that night would gather around his heart. It would build to the point that his heart would be crushed under the weight of it all.

Because he has been there, he understands when OUR heart is crushed.

The book of Hebrews expresses it this way:

> **Seeing that we have a great high priest, that is passed into the heavens, Jesus the Son of God, let us hold fast our profession.**
>
> **For we have not an high priest which cannot be touched with the feelings of our infirmities; but was in all points tempted like we are, yet without sin.**

Let us therefore come boldly unto the throne of grace, that we may obtain mercy, and find grace to help in time of need. (Heb. 4:14–16, KJV)

The most literal and accurate application of this verse is that when we are faced with a temptation or a snare that would entangle us, Jesus has already faced it and overcome it without succumbing to sin. Because he has already overcome, we can go to the throne in prayer when faced with a temptation and find the grace we need to overcome it.

But I think it can go even deeper than that. When it says he was "touched by the feeling of our infirmities," I believe it means that everything our heart feels, he has already felt. Every trauma of the human experience he has experienced up close and personally. It may seem like what we are going through is unique to us, but he, too, has gone through it.

No one can point a finger at God and say, "You don't understand what I am going through. You don't know what I have had to face."

As I have said before and will probably repeat; *he has already been to Gethsemane.* His heart has already been crushed for us. He understands our deepest pain. When our world has seemingly crumbled and is in ruins, there is one who knows what we are going through.

It is there in the arms of Jesus that we find comfort and relief when there seems to be none.

We have walked together into the garden of Gethsemane. We have seen the forces arrayed against our Lord. Hopefully, you have gotten a sense of the anguish he experienced. We have witnessed the Lord's response and resolution in the midst of the struggle.

The question we now face is: How will we respond when our hearts are crushed?

PART TWO

Have You Had a Gethsemane?

<hr />

**The Lord is nigh unto them
that are of a broken heart;
And saveth such as be of a contrite spirit.**

—Psalm 34:18 (KJV)

CHAPTER 6

Facing a Personal Gethsemane

"It would be so easy to just quit and die." The awareness suddenly dawned on Del. "It would be like hitting a light switch. Just give up and I would be gone." It was time to do business with God.

Del Land was the typical sixteen-year-old boy. He was an okay student; nothing spectacular. He studied as a means to be eligible to play school sports. He lived for sports. Ellijay was a small town in the north Georgia mountains, but many in the community felt he was an outstanding athlete.

His grandfather, Oscar Land, was a preacher, and Del grew up in church. In 1971, during the spring revival at their church, Del accepted Christ as his Savior and was saved.

Their church was of the "country" variety. They emphasized evangelism, but really didn't do much to disciple someone after they were saved. As a result, although Del had a relationship with the Lord, he was not growing in that relationship. He basically would be called a "nominal" Christian. Playing sports was still his all-consuming passion.

Del's father, Delmar Land, played piano for an up-and-coming gospel quartet, the Ambassadors. They were just beginning to gain notice and popularity. The future looked bright for them.

To help ends meet, they owned a dry cleaning and clothing shop. In the small mountain town, they would make deliveries of dry cleaning to homes. To do that they owned an Econoline van with clothing racks running through the van. The engine sat between the driver's seat and the passenger seat. There were no seat belts in the van.

On September 5, 1974, Delmar picked up Del and his ten-year-old sister, Susan, from school in the business van. They turned onto Highway 5 and headed home.

There were several roadhouses scattered up and down Highway 5. There were no national "drunk driving" campaigns back then. You never heard much about it, but with so many roadhouses dotting the landscape, it made that particular stretch of road a dangerous place.

While the Lands were heading home, three friends were helping their drunk friend to his car at one of the roadhouses. They kind of "poured" him into his car and walked back inside, while the man fumbled with his keys and finally got the car started. He pulled out onto the highway and took off. The man behind the wheel already had three DUIs.

It wasn't long before his car was traveling in excess of 100 MPH. Later, investigators would surmise that he probably passed out and slid down into the floorboard of the car as it hurtled like a missile down the road.

Much of what happened next would be a little hazy to Del, but there were some things that stuck out in his mind.

As the car approached a curve in the road, Del and his father had been having a "discussion" about a new car. Del was sitting with his feet propped up on the dashboard and had been fussing at his dad over the fact that he was sixteen and did not have a car yet. Delmar was trying to explain to him that the family couldn't afford another vehicle at that time.

Coming out of the curve, it seemed to Del that time hit the pause button and everything began to move in slow motion. Coming at them was a vehicle in their lane. He remembered thinking, *There's no way we're going to miss that car.*

Delmar tried to cut the van to the left, but there was no time to avoid the crash.

In the slow-motion instance before collision, Del remembered thinking that he didn't see a driver behind the wheel of the oncoming vehicle.

The impact knocked the van backward. Del and Susan were ejected from the van. Del landed in a ditch. He never lost consciousness, but in the resulting shock, he wasn't quite sure what had just happened.

Sadly, the drunk driver was killed on impact.

The first thing Del became aware of was hearing his dad screaming out, "Help me! Help me! Help me!" Delmar was pinned in the crushed van, caught by the engine block. The van had caught fire and was slowly turning into an inferno.

Del's first instinct was, *I've got to go help Dad*, but for some reason, he couldn't get his legs to work. He looked down at his legs and saw that one was twisted in an unnatural position. The other one had a bone sticking out of it. He was a little surprised that he couldn't feel any pain.

Not quite realizing that in the next few weeks he would be fighting for his life, the silly thought that flashed through his mind was, *I don't guess I'm going to be able to play in the game this week.*

This was the situation Del found himself in. He is in a ditch, watching his father burn alive, and is totally unable to help. He felt totally helpless.

People were beginning to stop and were trying to help, but the fire was too hot to approach the van.

Along this stretch of the mountain community, there were no water lines. Fire departments in the area had no tanker trucks to bring water. The only one who had a tanker truck was the Forestry Service. There was no way to extinguish the flames.

A Coke truck had stopped along with the dozens of other people trying to help. The driver jumped out with a fire extinguisher, but the extinguisher ran empty after only a couple of minutes. The fire roared back ferociously. People were frantically trying anything; grabbing Coke containers to try to douse the flames, but once again they could not even approach it because of the heat.

Up to this point, the people who had stopped were concentrated on the van and no one knew about Del and Susan. Del was taking all this in as he helplessly watched from the ditch. Finally, someone came across Del and called out to the others. A search began and they finally found Susan.

One of the men who had stopped, Hyatt Tankersley, was trying to shield Del from the horrific scene playing out in front of them, but Del knew enough to know what was going on.

By the time the Forestry Service Tanker finally arrived, the damage had already been done. It took a little longer for the ambulance to show up.

With the fire finally extinguished they were able to extricate Delmar from the van. While this was going on, paramedics were getting Del and Susan ready for transport. Today paramedics would never use an air splint on an open wound. In 1974, it was different. The paramedics began to put an air splint on his decimated leg.

Up until this point, the shock had prevented Del from feeling any pain. Everything changed when they put the air splint on his leg. All of a sudden, Del was consumed by an overwhelming and excruciating pain like nothing he had ever experienced.

All three were loaded into the ambulance and sped to the small hospital in Ellijay, where Del's mother, Evelyn, met them. The sight that met Evelyn was horrendous. Susan was in hysterics, Del was in excruciating pain, and not a sound was coming from Delmar.

The doctor on staff that night, Dr. Fernandez, trying to assess the situation told the nurses to cut Del's pants off so he could examine him. Del illogically responded, "But they are my favorite blue jeans."

It quickly became evident to Dr. Fernandez that their small hospital was not equipped to handle three such dire cases, and that time was running out. He turned to the ambulance drivers who were still nearby.

"You've got to get them to Kennestone Hospital immediately. You have about forty-five minutes to get them there." Kennestone was in Marietta, Georgia, over fifty miles away with only a two-lane road connecting them.

The driver responded, "That's impossible! There's no way we can get to Kennestone in forty-five minutes!"

Dr. Hernandez answered, "You *have* to." Then pointing to Susan, "If you don't, she will slowly bleed out. It's a matter of their survival."

As they were loading them back in the ambulance and Evelyn was about to climb in for the trip, Dr. Hernandez gave her the stark evaluation, "I don't know if your children will make it or not. Your husband *will not* survive."

What followed was the most harrowing race against time imaginable. The ambulance virtually flew down the road with the clock quickly tick-tick-ticking. At times the ambulance would careen precariously. At one curve, it seemed like the ambulance might overturn, but righted itself and continued on its perilous journey.

Somewhere around Highway 92 in Woodstock, Delmar lifted his head and asked the nurse, "Are Del and Susan all right?"

She responded, "They are going to be fine."

At that Delmar laid his head back and passed away, leaving the torment he was experiencing behind.

Finally, the paramedics did the impossible. They landed at Kennestone Hospital in approximately thirty-seven minutes. With just eight minutes to spare, they had given Del and Susan their best chance of survival.

In retrospect, the quick actions of Dr. Fernandez and the paramedics probably saved their lives, but the night was not over for Susan and Del. Susan would end up in a full body cast and Del would undergo the first of many surgeries on his legs as he fought for his life.

As they were prepping Del for surgery, the lead surgeon spoke to Del, "I'm Dr. Sturkey. This is Dr. Paine and Dr. Mckinnon. They will be assisting me. We are going to take *good care* of you."

Del looked down at his legs then back at the doctors and responded, "Seriously?"

The accident occurred at 6:16 PM. Del was in surgery from 8:00 PM to 3:00 AM.

The next morning, following the surgery, Dr. Sturkey determined that the circulation had stopped in Del's left leg. They would have to take serious measures to try and correct the situation.

The following days and weeks would see Del in and out of awareness as he went through a series of surgeries. Over a period of ten to eleven days, Del would undergo at least six surgeries. In fact, his most critical plight lay just ahead.

The decision had been made not to tell Del yet that his dad was gone, but Del already knew without being told that he had died. With everything else he had to undergo, he had to process the fact that his dad, who was his hero, was gone for good.

On day eleven of his ordeal, gangrene set in. They began to talk about amputation.

On September 17, the day the amputation was scheduled, Del had gotten a hair dryer and tried to warm up his foot. When the doctor came in and found his foot warm, he was surprised until he realized what Del had done. He had a good chuckle at what Del had done, and the amputation proceeded as planned.

This was the part that was the most difficult for Del. He had always been an athlete. He loved playing all sports. Now he felt he was closing out that part of his life. In succession, he had lost his dad, his leg, and now any chance of playing again.

Up until this point, he had experienced an amazing, supernatural peace that whispered to him that everything was going to be all right. It was a peace that had strengthened him through this ordeal.

But now, everything began piling up on him. All his blood's clotting factors were gone due to his almost bleeding out after the amputation. He worried about how his mom could run the businesses and pay the bills on her own. The kicker was when they brought a wheelchair in and they began to teach him how to get in and out of a wheelchair.

"What is this for?" Del asked.

The doctor replied bluntly, "We don't think you'll ever be able to walk again."

Two weeks out from the accident, the peace he experienced was replaced by depression. He became extremely angry. He didn't want to see anybody. When the deacons from Pleasant Grove Baptist Church, who had been so good to visit every day, came by, he wanted nothing to do with them.

That was when the realization dawned on him that if he gave up the will to live, he would just slip away. It would be as easy as flipping a light switch.

This isn't right, he thought. *I've got to get serious about doing some business with God.*

Del had, due to his lack of understanding the scriptures, operated under a mistaken notion about God. He thought that when people said that *God would go with you in troubles* that it meant God would keep troubles from *coming your way.* If a tragedy occurred, it had to be punishment for sin. He was struggling with the question: What did I do to deserve this?

The logical next question that arose was: If I am being punished, why did it have to affect my dad, Susan, and our entire family? The more he prayed and wrestled with it, the more it just didn't make sense.

Del was mad at God.

After a long struggle, Del heard clearly from God. It came as a sudden impression upon his heart. It was not the answer he was looking for.

While pouring out his complaint to the Lord, Del in his frustration cried out, "WHY ME?"

Instantaneously, the Lord responded, "WHY NOT YOU?"

Was he some kind of privileged person that he had to be sheltered and shielded from any and all heartache? Was he so special that he should walk through life without a care in the world?

That moment was the turning point for Del. It was the realization that God had to have a plan for his life. It answered the question, "Do I want to live, or do I want to die?" He came to the conclusion that he wanted to live to experience God's plan for his life.

That was the starting point of his mental recovery.

It would not be easy. There was a physical, mental, and emotional aspect to his recovery. Susan would suffer years of mental anguish. Del would experience the embarrassment of returning to school and having to use a walker. In his mind, the once great athlete was reduced to a shell of his former glory. It was hard to take.

He eventually would walk again with the use of a prosthetic leg.

Two years after the accident, he would begin dating his future wife, Tamara. Back then, no one ever suggested counseling, and Tamara became the person he could talk things out with. There was no greater match for Del than Tamara.

He would eventually move his church membership to a church that not only emphasized evangelism, but also discipleship. He began a lifelong study of the Word of God that would help to change his outlook.

Full recovery would take years.

* * * * *

I did not know Del back then. I never saw the angry young man. I never knew the young man who would fight to regain something of a normal life. I never knew the Del who had to wage a spiritual battle to hear a word from God.

I first met Del thirty-two years after the accident when I moved to Ellijay. The man I know is rock solid in his faith. He is one of the best Bible teachers I have heard. He has a keen insight into the Word of God. He is a man with a tender heart that is often moved to the point where he gets choked up when talking about the Lord.

He has been a man of service to his Lord, church, and community. Whether it has been in teaching a Sunday school class or serving as a county commissioner, he has left his mark on his community. He has also on occasion given talks in the high school, telling his story, and warning the kids of the dangers of drinking and driving.

He loves his family and has been successful in the business world.

Except for his prosthetic leg, you would see no sign that the tragedy had ever occurred.

I never saw his struggles. What I saw was the work of grace that had taken place within this man.

September 5, 1974, marked the beginning of his "Gethsemane experience." I use that term to indicate an event or series of events where the pressures build upon the heart pushing a person seemingly to the end of human endurance. It will have one of two effects on a person. It can make them stronger, or it can destroy them.

Let me be quick to clarify; you will *never* have to face anything that compares to what Jesus faced in the Garden of Gethsemane. Anything we face in life pales in comparison to what he suffered that night. In that sense, it might not seem like an accurate word to use in our experience.

But when a person is going through a time of heart break, it will *seem* to them to be of the same magnitude as Gethsemane.

It becomes our *own personal Gethsemane.*

It is where the heart is crushed

No one is immune to the potential of having their heart torn apart. A person may feel like what they are going through is somehow unique, but it is a common experience. As strange as it may seem, being able to feel pain is a blessing in disguise. Who wants to live a life so coldhearted and detached that they never "feel" anything?

As Gethsemane (the olive press) was the perfect word to depict the place where Jesus suffered, so there is no better word to describe what happens to the human heart than to say it is *crushed.*

When a person faces their own personal Gethsemane, it becomes *the single event that drastically alters their life.* It will change their outlook. For better or for worse, how they view things will be different.

It can even *change your personality.* How often has a carefree spirit become guarded after a traumatic incident? A trusting soul can become innately suspicious.

Your walk with God will be different than before. It can make that bond closer and more intimate, or if their faith is shallow, it can cause a person to question God.

In the "worst reaction" category, it can bring depression and add drudgery to life. To a person who has absolutely no relationship with

God, it can bring about a feeling of helplessness. Self is no longer sufficient to handle the pressure.

There is, however, a marvelous message for those facing a Gethsemane.

Jesus is found where the heart is crushed

Jesus understands exactly what I am facing. He has already experienced every heartbreak in life that we do. When God took upon himself the flesh of man, he *identified with us* in all things. He knows what we are going through, and he cares for our well-being. I may not understand your situation for I may not have experienced what you have. Jesus, however, is fully aware of all the little details of our life.

He is there in the furnace with us. We do not stand alone. At the risk of repeating myself again, *he has already been to Gethsemane.* He has gone through it for us.

I was leafing through a songbook and ran across an old gospel song I haven't heard in years. Nobody really knows who wrote the song. It is entitled "Is Not This the Land of Beulah," and the last verse speaks to the truth that he has walked that path before us.

> Oh, the cross has wondrous glory!
> Oft I've proved this to be true,
> When I'm in the way so narrow,
> I can see a pathway through;
> And how sweetly Jesus whispers,
> Take the cross thou needst not fear,
> *For I've trod the way before thee,*
> *And the GLORY lingers near.*

As we travel that path with a broken heart, we become aware of one that has passed before. With each step, we came smell a fragrance of that glory lingering behind. We come to realize that we are following in the footsteps that he has already walked.

Not only has he walked before us, he is walking WITH us. Sometimes he has to stop, lift us up, and carry us. He leaves us a breath of his glory not only when we are happy and rejoicing, but when he has to carry us.

He knows of our heartache, and he understands.

Not only is he aware of what we are experiencing, but *he has provided the means* whereby we can be healed emotionally, spiritually, mentally, and physically. No hand can bring comfort like his. No arm can offer strength like his.

There is always hope when you add God into the equation.

Strength can be found in the truth of God's word

Unfortunately, many people are plagued by an erroneous view of God. They, like Del, will feel that they are to be shielded from any tragedy. When troubles, which are inevitable in life, do happen, then they feel like it must be a punishment for some great sin that they have done. This is the same argument that Job's three friends made to him. If misfortune arises, then God must be punishing you because of sin.

Others will point their finger at God and say, "You let me down."

It doesn't help when some "prosperity preachers" make it sound as if the reward for following God will come in *this* life. Tell that to the apostles, who to a man faced persecution for their faith.

God never promised to keep tragedies from coming our way, but he did say *he would walk through them with us*. In fact, he promised us peace through the tribulation.

Behold, the hour cometh, yea, is now come, that ye shall be scattered, every man to his own, and ye shall leave me alone: and yet I am not alone, because the Father is with me.

These things have I spoken unto you that ye might have peace. *In the world ye shall have tribulation*: **But be of good cheer; I have overcome the world.** (Jn 16:32–33, KJV)

These words were spoken by Jesus to the disciples mere minutes before they entered the Garden of Gethsemane. He did not prevent the disciples from entering into Gethsemane, but instead said that they could experience a supernatural peace as they walked through Gethsemane.

When faced with an overwhelming tragedy, *don't wait for understanding.* Just continue to trust God. In the story of Job, there is no indication that Job ever understood why everything happened to him. He never saw the spiritual contention that took place in heaven concerning him. Even though he likely questioned some things in his mind, his Faith never wavered.

There *was* an effect on Job, however. His walk with God was strengthened. His relationship with God deepened. He came out of it a better man.

A personal self-examination

Though my trials might not compare with others in their gravity, I have not been immune to them. In examining my own experiences, I have come to a few conclusions. *I am a product of all that has happened to me.* Those times of testing and heartache have molded me into the person I am today. They have affected me emotionally and spiritually. My outlook on life, my relationship with my Lord, and even how I respond to other people have been shaped by those times of suffering.

By looking closely at myself (which can be a very difficult thing to do) I have come to a few conclusions. First, *any strength I have was developed during times of suffering.* My faith would never have needed to be strong if I had never been tested. It was during those times that my faith was exercised and grew.

If I have any spiritual insight, it was born in the furnace. How often have I been going through some of my old study note or been reading my Bible and came to the realization that a particular insight I had with scripture came to me during a time of struggle.

That leads me to a further conclusion. If there is any goodness in me at all, *it came from Jesus.*

In retrospect, though I would never want to repeat those times, *I thank God for the trials.* It was there I saw his hand in action. It was there he proved his Word to be true. I can testify to the fact that he is faithful because I have been through the storm and I saw him there.

The reason I can be confident of his care during times of trouble is because he has experienced the pain of Gethsemane. He understands and he cares.

In the chapters that follow, we will take a look at specific times in our lives when our heart becomes traumatized. In all of them, we will see a Savior, who has walked that way before us; the one who knelt in that garden and suffered for our sake.

* * * * *

Although I didn't know Del back then, I have since discovered some connections and in fact was aware of the incident.

My grandfather, Rev. Ralph Foster, and his Grandfather Oscar were both preachers who traveled in the same circles.

Also, in 1974, my brother Johnny and I were both members of Antioch Baptist Church. Our pastor, Dr. Gene Winfrey, was driving back home from a meeting and came upon the accident. He was one of the ones who got out of their cars to try and help.

The next Sunday he shared the experience with the congregation in his sermon. I don't really recall what his sermon was about, but I do remember it was a very moving service. The altars were filled and God did a work in many people's lives. It was only later, after I had met Del, that my brother and I put two and two together and realized that Del was the young son lying in the ditch that Gene had talked about.

So, while Del was fighting for his life in a hospital, his story was already having an effect on people.

I once asked Del a question. "Del, we know that all things are not good, but that Romans 8:28 (KJV) says *All things work together for good to them that love God, to them who are the called according to his purpose.* In thinking back on it, what do you see as good that came out of all of it?"

He began his answer by saying, "Of course if I had a choice I would not choose to go through it again." Then he began to list several things that came out of the incident.

He spoke of the immediate attention it brought locally to the problem of drunk driving and that stretch of road with all the roadhouses. Ben Whitaker became county commissioner and took the county dry for several years. He yanked the licenses of the roadhouses along that stretch and closed them down. "No telling how many lives were saved by those actions," he said.

He spoke of the people it impacted; the many people who had come up to him and said that the accident had caused them to examine the way they were living their lives and made drastic changes.

He spoke of the many times he has publicly shared his story to warn young people of the dangers of drinking and driving.

He spoke of the way that now he has a deeper appreciation of each minute of life.

He then made a simple statement that I thought was profound in its simplicity.

"Looking back, everything I see is good. I don't see a thing about my life that isn't good."

CHAPTER 7

The Testing of Faith

The morning was just about to break. The sun, which was just below the horizon, cast a pinkish red glow across the clouds that were just skirting the rise of the earth. The wind was bringing all the old familiar smells as the fishing boat gently rocked in the calm waters off shore.

This was the life Peter had grown up in. It was the way of life he loved. On any normal day, he would have sat back and savored every moment. The peacefulness of the coming dawn coupled with his familiarity of the routine should have made this an enjoyable time of reflection on how good his life was.

But this was not a normal day. Dark thoughts crowded into Peter's mind dispelling any thought of peaceful reflection. In fact, Peter didn't really want to be thinking at all. He wanted to just go about the routine of fishing without being bothered by thinking about things that could not be changed. The embarrassment of his failure kept popping up like an unwanted relative that you just couldn't get to go home. He wondered if his fishing companions, men that had walked with him for three years following the Master, knew just how badly he had failed the test.

He was great at talking, but when it came down to actually standing boldly with Jesus, he had succumbed to fear. Try as he might, he couldn't seem to erase that shame from his mind.

Finally, Peter gave up trying and sat down in the boat and let the memory of those final moments take over his consciousness, running amok and taking his thoughts to places they did not want to go.

First, there had been the headlong flight out of Gethsemane. He did not realize he could run that fast, but gripped by an overwhelming fear like none he had ever known, he had made his escape and stood trying to catch his breath in the moonlight.

What was happening? Peter's mind couldn't quite grasp what had just happened. This was not what he expected. He had believed that Jesus was the Messiah. He had never envisioned anything like this happening. He had to find out what was happening with the Master.

It was the temple guard who had taken him, Peter thought. *They will take him to Caiaphas.*

Stealthily, he began to make his way back toward Zion's hill, where Caiaphas's palace stood. He arrived not sure of what to do next. How could he gain entrance without drawing attention to himself? The last thing he wanted to happen was to be recognized by anyone.

As he stood there, he noticed John inside the gate. *That's right,* he thought. *John has connections with the high priest.*

After trying several times, he finally got John's attention. John spoke to the gatekeeper and began to beckon to Peter. Once inside they began to quietly confer with each other.

"Do you know what is happening?" Peter inquired.

"The Master is going to be brought before Caiaphas. I don't know if that hearing has begun yet." John responded. "I'm going to go speak with some people to see if I can find out what is going on."

"Let me know when you find out anything."

"I will. Stay here and try to be inconspicuous."

Peter moved into the courtyard. There seemed to be quite a few people gathered in groups all around the courtyard. Peter wondered that there were so many people milling around at this time of night. He shivered with the briskness of the night and wandered over to where a group of people were standing around a fire to warm up.

He started rubbing his hands together in front of it, trying to get the circulation going again.

He noticed a servant girl scrutinizing him. It was an uncomfortable kind of glare. Peter kept trying to divert his eyes away from her; his apprehension growing each time he glanced her way.

"You were with him. You were with this Jesus. You are one of them." The words were coming from the servant girl.

Peter looked around. Everyone's attention seemed to be focused all of a sudden on him.

"What are you talking about?" Peter blurted out. "I don't know this man, whatever his name was."

Peter moved as quickly as he could away from this group to another. He was followed by a second maid who had overheard the conversation.

"I saw you with him!" she trumpeted loud enough for everyone in the courtyard to hear. "You are one of his disciples!"

"I never met this man you are talking about!" Peter fumbled. "Just leave me alone."

Another man sidled up to him. "Listen to his accent," he intoned. "It is Galilean! He must be one of them."

The panic seized ahold of Peter, and he began spewing a torrent of the vilest vitriol and curses that one could imagine. This was the type of language a fisherman used, but that he had not used since meeting the Master. He concluded his tirade by shouting, "I'm telling you, I do not know the man!"

Immediately, Peter heard a rooster crow. With a start, the words Jesus had spoken in the upper room came flooding back to Peter, "Before the rooster crows, you shall deny me three times."

There was a sudden movement of people, as the guard came through leading Jesus from his holding cell to where he would be interrogated by Caiaphas. The eyes of the Lord sought out Peter.

There was nothing like that look. It seemed to bore right through Peter; exposing his very soul. Shame flooded through him, and he turned and fled from the courtyard, out the gate as quickly as he could.

Once outside by himself, he collapsed. The grief overwhelmed him till he cried like he had never cried in his life.

Peter shook the memories out of his head, bringing him back to the present. Here in the fishing boat, the guilt almost made him start crying again, but he stifled it so that his companions wouldn't see it.

What made his failure even more glaring was the events that followed Jesus's death. First there were the reports of the women who followed the Lord. They spoke of the tomb being empty, visions of angels, and of the Lord himself speaking with Mary.

Then the most amazing thing had happened. Jesus had appeared to the disciples who were gathered together. He spoke with them. He sat down and ate with them.

There was no question that he had died.

There was no question that he was alive again.

The joy Peter felt was bittersweet. He couldn't get over the fact that he had failed. He looked deep within himself and came to a conclusion. *He was not worthy to be called one of his disciples.*

That had caused Peter to come to a decision. He had to go on with his life, so he would return to the fishing profession. It was what he knew. It was what he was comfortable with. He just didn't feel like he was "cut out" for the life of a preacher. Someone else would have to carry this message. He did not have the abilities to. He had merely been fooling himself for three years.

After announcing it to his compatriots, he managed to convince several of them to join him, Including James and John. They were experienced with fishing and would be valuable to his new enterprise.

Now here they were. After launching into their new partnership, they had nothing to show for it. They had toiled all night and had not caught a single fish.

As the sun gradually began to top the horizon, the shoreline came more into focus. They could distantly make out a figure standing on the shore. There was something about the way he was gazing in their direction that caught Peter's attention.

A voice echoed out across the waters, "Have you caught any fish?"

It was James who thundered back, "No. It hasn't been a very good night."

"Cast your net on the other side." The familiarity of this caught their attention as the disciples looked quickly at each other.

"Let's do as he says, men," John intoned as they scrambled to lower nets off of the other side. Something was beginning to whelm up inside of Peter, as all of a sudden, there was a lurch on the nets indicating a surge of fish had hit the nets.

The realization hit John who turned to Peter and exclaimed, "It's the Lord!"

A shiver ran up Peter's spine and ended in his eyes when he heard those words. "Let's go to him! Come on, let's row!"

"We've got to get the fish into the boat first."

"Well, hurry! Hurry!"

As the men began to struggle with the nets, Peter continued to gaze at the figure on the shore. A longing to be with him was beginning to overwhelm impatient Peter.

This is taking too long, he thought as they continued to draw the nets. *I have to get to him NOW!*

Drawing his garment around him, Peter dove into the water and began swimming. His mind was consumed by one thing: *I must get to him!*

As the boat approached shore, the first thing the disciples noticed was the smell of fish cooking. John suddenly realized that he was famished. As hungry as he was, that aroma was intoxicating.

They set about securing the boat, before they disembarked. John looked over toward the shore, and there he saw Peter sitting down gazing upon the face of the Lord. Jesus was tending a fire upon which there was already some fish; enough for all of them.

Jesus looked toward them, and called out, "Come and dine."

Apparently, everyone else felt like John did, for there was a mad scramble to get out of the boat and come by the fire.

After such a frustrating night, there was nothing so satisfying as being in the presence of the Master, feasting on the fish he had provided for them. John couldn't help but notice that the Lord's attention was turned to Peter.

Gesturing toward the fishing boat, the nets, and the catch of fish the Lord addressed Peter, "Simon, son of Jonas, do you love me more than these things?"

Peter dropped his head a little, the remembrance of his failure caused him to avoid the Lord's gaze. How could he claim to love him after denying him in such a public manner?

What he managed to answer was, "Lord, you know that I am fond of you."

Then the Lord responded, "Then feed my sheep." Peter understood perfectly what the Lord was saying to him. He didn't need to go into detail. As usual, the Lord could get his point across without going into detail. He just as well could have said, "Fishing is not the life I have chosen for you. Your purpose in life is to feed my sheep."

Jesus spoke a little softer this time, "Simon, son of Jonas, do you love me?"

The fact that Jesus repeated the same question grieved Peter. "Lord, you know that I am fond of you."

After a long pause, Jesus, with as much gravity as he could, asked, "Peter, are you even fond of me?"

With that, Peter's stubborn will was broken, "Lord, you know all things. You know my heart. You know that I love you."

Jesus answered him, "I am appointing you to feed my sheep. When you were young, you chose your own way. There will come a time when another shall bind you and take you against your will."

Peter understood what the Lord was saying. Following Jesus would eventually lead to his death. It didn't matter to Peter. He had failed once before. The feeling of love that was expanding within his very heart demanded a devotion from him, and he would not fail him a second time.

* * * * *

Faith, by its very nature, is intangible. You cannot produce something solid, hold it in your hands, and say, "This is my faith." It doesn't require proof. It is, however, every bit as real as something solid.

When I say that faith doesn't require proof, that does not mean it is baseless. *All faith is based on something.* Is what it is based on dependable or untrustworthy? Will what it is based on stand the test of time, or is it based on a fleeting fad?

Just as important to understand is that *faith has an object.* Upon what is your faith placed? Is it placed on something solid, or something shifting? Is it time tested and is it strong enough to stand?

All faith will be tested. It is inevitable. There *will* be things occur in your life that will call into question the very foundation of what you believe. This doesn't mean that there is something wrong with you. It is a natural part of life.

It is important to note that a test *cannot* shake a genuine faith. It will merely reveal what "sort" of faith that you have. Those characteristics of faith we just talked about will be uncovered by your test.

It will show what your faith is *based* on. Is it based on the time-tested Word of God, or is it based on a "feeling" that can change over time? For century upon century and countless millennium, God's Word has upheld believers in time of crisis. It has proven itself reliable. I can personally testify to the fact that it has sustained me through the toughest curve balls life can throw at you.

Testing will also show *where* your faith is placed. If I place faith in myself, whatever my abilities might be, there will be some things that pop up out of my control. If my abilities cannot handle it, what does that do to my faith?

If, however, my faith is *placed in God*, it is placed in much more capable hands than mine. Let me be more specific. If it is placed in *the person of the Lord Jesus Christ*, then I am placing my faith in the one who has already weathered the storm.

When a crisis of faith does occur, it can be absolutely devastating to the individual. It will be a desolation of the soul, for it will strike at the very bedrock of a person's existence.

What triggers a crisis of faith?

A crisis of faith can be brought on *when a tragedy occurs*. The unthinkable actually happens. Your worst fears come to pass.

A young mother is busy around the house, thinking her young child is taking a nap. Unknown to her, the child has woken up and wandered outside the house and into the woods. She becomes hopelessly lost, and before the mother even knows she is gone, the young child meets up with a sad end.

Or a child can disappear.

Trust me when I say that although nothing like this has ever happened to me personally, it is extremely difficult to even *write* about something like this occurring. I can't imagine what it must be like, but I have known families that have gone through similar experiences.

It is easy to understand how a person's faith would be challenged in a situation like that.

Something else that can launch a challenge to your faith is when *things don't go according to a preconceived idea*. We have our own thoughts about how God is supposed to work in our lives. He doesn't always move the way we think he should.

I heard of an elderly preacher once that made the claim that, like Simeon in Luke 2, he had been given a promise from the Lord that he should not taste death until he saw the Lord's return. That man is now dead, and the Lord hasn't returned yet.

I would never question a man's sincerity, and this man no doubt had a deep love for the Lord. But he was wrong about that claim to a promise. The Lord *has* promised to return, and he *will* return, but his word says that no man knows the day nor the hour of his return. This preacher probably had such a strong desire to be alive when the Lord returned that he convinced himself he had a promise from the Lord.

Suppose a young Christian not yet grounded in the Word of God saw this claim as a "sign" that the Lord's return was imminent. When it was not fulfilled in the manner he thought it should be, it could cause him to question if his promise to return was true. His faith would be in question.

A challenge to a person's faith could also occur when, in his efforts to serve the Lord, he does not meet with success. "I was trying to serve you." He might say. "But, where were you, Lord? I didn't see your hand."

There are times when our own desires will convince us that something is God's will. When it turns out not to be His will, it could result in a crisis of faith. If a person's faith is not grounded "rock solid" on the Word of God, then it can be shaken.

A solid faith will stand sure, even if we mistake God's will.

Another trigger that can cause a crisis of faith is when a person, like Peter, experiences *a personal failure*. Whether it is the failure of a marriage, the failure of an endeavor, or outright sin in a person's life, personal failure can have a devastating effect on a person's life.

It is human nature to always shift the blame to someone or something else when we fall short. Unfortunately, sometimes a person will want to blame God. They will react like Adam after the fall. He pointed his finger at God and said, "The woman YOU gave me enticed me and I ate the fruit!" In so doing, he tried to pass the blame onto not only Eve, but to God himself for making the woman in the first place. (I can hear women all across the world saying, "That is SO like a man!")

Instead of realizing that the failure was of our own making, we strike out at others, doubling down on the devastation, and making the situation a whole lot worse.

Failing the test

When faith is put to the test and fails, it can affect a person both spiritually and emotionally. The agony that is experienced can have a Gethsemane feel to it. It seems as if it could go on forever. The results can have dire consequences.

First of all, it can result in a person *doubting their salvation*. Nothing disrupts peace of mind like never being sure that you are saved. Not only will doubt destroy your peace of mind, but it incapacitates, leaving your spiritual life lethargic.

I'll have to confess that this is something I don't quite understand. I have never had a serious doubt about my salvation since the day I got saved. To me it is straightforward. When I trusted him, I placed my salvation in *his* hands. It is now out of my hands for I entrusted it to him. Why should I doubt *his* hands?

I have come to discover, however, that at some point most Christians will experience periods where they question whether or not they have been saved. Most overcome this as they grow in the Word and grow in grace. Where it becomes dangerous, is when the doubt can't be shaken.

I have known of individuals, choice servants of God, who were overcome by doubt. The sad result was that it effectively ended their service to God.

Another result of failing the test of faith is when a person totally turns from the faith and *denies God's existence.* I have never personally known someone who was a believer and later turned their back on God and became a non-believer. I have serious doubts that someone who had a genuine relationship with God could ever turn around and deny his existence. Even people who backslid and fell into sin still retained a belief in God.

You might be wondering what I would say about someone who would do that. I would point you to what John said in the scriptures:

> **Little children, it is the last time: and as ye have heard that antichrist shall come, even now are there many antichrists; whereby we know that it is the last time.**
>
> **They went out from among us; but they were not of us, for if they had been of us, they would no doubt have continued with us: but they went out, that they might be made manifest that they were not all of us.** (1 Jn 2:18–19, KJV)

John spoke of many during the first century who came on the scene in the spirit of antichrist. They opposed the work of Christ and stood in opposition to the church. John then made a startling admission. They sprang out of our ranks. They once identified themselves as believers and had attached themselves to a group of believers. They left, but took things a bit farther. They arrayed themselves in total opposition to Christ.

John's analysis of these people was that that had never been genuine believers. It had all been a façade. He concluded that had they been actual believers, there would have been no question but that they would have remained believers.

I am in agreement with John. If a person can "claim" to be a Christian and then turn from Christ and become apostate, there was something fundamentally flawed about their "faith" to begin with. They had no real relationship with God. If they had a relationship with him, they would have known that there was someone there to have a relationship with. They would be aware of his existence. Since, however, their false faith had nothing to root itself in, they questioned his very existence.

The apostate's need is to come to the Word of God, accept Christ, and BEGIN his relationship with God.

Perhaps the ultimate result of a crisis of faith is that it *defeats your service for the Lord.* That is what was in danger of happening to Peter in the story we opened this chapter with. When Peter said, "I go a fishing," he wasn't talking about just an afternoon by the Creekside. In effect, he was saying, "I'm returning to my old occupation; my old way of life." He was giving up on service to the Lord.

His decision affected others; influencing them to follow in his stead. It's true that every decision we make affects other people in some form. We do not live our lives in a vacuum. Every step we take can influence for good or bad those around us.

Bear this in mind. His decision occurred *after* he had seen the risen Lord. He knew the truth of the claim that Christ had risen from the dead. There was no questioning the validity of the claim. He had seen the Lord. He heard him speak.

It is a safe assumption to believe that it was his feelings of guilt over his failure that caused him to take this course. He certainly would have felt unworthy to take the mantle of Apostleship. Then again, he may have begun to *doubt his own abilities* to serve the Master.

It is true that on our own we cannot effectively serve the Lord. We need his help. When, however, we use our lack of abilities as an excuse not to serve him, we are really doubting *his* ability to use us.

The Lord had to address Peter's choice. That is what his questioning of Peter was all about. He was asking him, "Do you love me more than this profession; this lifestyle?" The fact that Jesus had to ask three times shows just how deep Peter's pain was.

That agony that Peter was experiencing, no doubt was as real to Peter as the Lord's own agony in the Garden. The difference was that Peter's pain was due to his own failure. Jesus's pain was *for* all of our failures and sins. The presence of the Lord only emphasized the difference.

Standing before him was the one who could say, "I suffered the agonies of Gethsemane for you!" No one could sympathize with Peter like the Lord could. He had been there. There remained only the correcting of Peter's course.

When Jesus answered, "Feed my sheep," he was telling him, "This is to be your new vocation. This is the plan I have for your life!" Peter was to be involved in the ministry as an Apostle. As such, he would help to set the foundation and the *doctrine* of the Church. He would be literally "feeding the sheep."

As it was with Peter, so it is with us. When we are experiencing suffering in our lives and think that no one understands, there stands one before us who says, "I understand. I suffered that pain for you. I have already been to Gethsemane. I care for you."

There is hope for those who fail the test

There is some encouraging news here for the person who has failed the testing of faith. *Peter was restored.* He could enjoy full fellowship with the Lord. He and the other apostles went on to turn the world upside down. *His failure did not disqualify him.*

There's no question that the Lord's confronting of Peter was not pleasant, but it was necessary. That confrontation was what brought Peter back to full restoration.

When Peter was restored and sitting at the feet of Jesus, he discovered something. Although the fishermen were pulling a huge catch of fish upon shore, there was already "fish on the fire" when Peter got there.

This illustrates an important point that we should always remember. Regardless of what we might bring to the table, whatever abilities or non-abilities we might have, Jesus has already provided all that we need. Do we feel like we are limited in talent? He has provided the means, the power, and the ability to serve him.

Perhaps you've been gifted with a talent. Maybe you've been given a wonderful singing voice. You need to understand that to effectively "communicate that message" in song takes more than just hitting the right notes. When HE empowers the singer, it turns from entertainment and becomes spiritual encouragement. He provides what the singer needs.

The same can be said for the preacher, teacher, or anyone in the service of God. He gives us the "fish on the fire" that we need to do the task.

What was required of Peter for his restoration was, first of all, an *acknowledgement* of his failure; the realization that left on his own, he had made a mess of things.

It next required *a turning his back on* the things that were preventing him from fulfilling God's will for his life. This is repentance, and is essential for restoration.

Finally, it took a *complete trusting of the Lord in all things.* It took a recognition of our total dependence upon the Lord for every aspect of our lives.

Peter went on to accomplish great things. You can also.

Is your faith being tested? Are you going through a Gethsemane of doubt?

The one who knelt in the Garden now stands before you. In his outstretched hands are all that you need to strengthen your faith and stand the test.

CHAPTER 8

The Testing of Sorrow

It was a ten-week ordeal. It was by far the most difficult period in the history of our family. It tried not just our spiritual strength, but also our emotions and our physical stamina.

My dad, Ralph "Jobo" Foster, was the one everyone in our family depended on. Whether, it was seeking advice or simply calling to talk about our day, Dad was the "hero" that we all looked to.

Dad didn't just grow old in a shell. He involved himself in people's lives. He showed an interest in what they were involved in and would become their greatest fans. If a neighbor kid had a basketball game, he would go and watch it.

This was especially true with his own grandchildren. When Kendall and Charter were in high school playing sports, he would do more than just go to every game. He went to every practice! Every day as they went through drills in football or practiced in baseball, they could see his van parked above the field watching. After practice, he might meet them with a Chick-Fil-A sandwich or something else and would often take them home.

All of Charter and Kendall's friends knew who he was. He had that ability to show interest in what they were doing, which was pretty amazing for someone in their eighties. I'm not saying he was "best buddies" with them. That would be a stretch. But his presence was known by them.

Early in life, Dad was known for his baseball playing abilities. He played professionally for several years in the minor leagues. While we were growing up, Dad was involved in coaching youth league teams.

But it was his faith in the Lord Jesus that truly made him stand out. He never preached a sermon, but his life was a sermon for all to see.

Dad loved gospel music. People loved hearing him sing songs like "I'm Bound for That City," and other gospel favorites. Whether it was singing with our family on my granddaddy's radio program, or singing in his church choir, he had a lifelong love affair with singing about his Lord.

To sum it all up, Dad was a much-loved man, and as, I mentioned before, he was our hero.

That's what made the last ten weeks in 2011 so difficult for us. We weren't ready to say, "Good bye."

At the age of eighty-five, Dad wrote off most of his aches and pains as just "getting old." Dad woke up and knew something wasn't right. He told Mom that he was going to go to the doctor's office. When Mom, who wasn't feeling well herself, mentioned something about going with him, he just said that wasn't necessary, and he would call her later.

He drove himself to the doctor's office. Once there, he almost didn't make it through the parking lot. When he finally made it into the doctor's office, they instantly knew that this was serious. They wasted no time in immediately rushing him to the emergency room. It was his heart.

I got a call at work from Mom. When she told me that Dad had been admitted to the hospital, I immediately got choked and began to tear up. Dad had been in the hospital before. A few years back, he'd had stints put in. He'd also had a kidney removed because of cancer. All procedures had been successful, and they had given no indication just how life threatening this present situation would be. But something came over me, and I instinctively knew that there was the possibility that we would be losing Dad.

I immediately left work and drove down to Kennestone Hospital. I lived and worked over an hour away. By the time I got there, Dad was in a room resting comfortably and seemed to be doing well. The rest of the family was there, and everything seemed to be in control. They would schedule a procedure in the next couple of days. In the meantime, the staff was taking good care of him.

When I left and drove home, I had the intention of returning to work and going back down when the procedure was performed.

The next morning, while getting ready for work, I got a call from my brother Johnny. All he could tell me was, "There's been an incident, and they're rushing Dad into emergency surgery."

After making a quick call to work, I flew out of the house and took off toward Marietta. Once again, the distance I lived from the hospital made for a very anxious trip. The whole trip down, not knowing what was going on, my mind was playing through all the possible scenarios, none of which seemed good.

It would take me well over an hour to get there, and just as I was taking the exit toward the hospital, Johnny called to say that they were bringing Dad out of surgery.

They related to me what had happened. Mom had just left the room. It was a blessing she hadn't been in the room to witness it. Dad had gotten out of bed and was talking to one of the nurses, when quite suddenly, he went into cardiac arrest and fell backward onto the bed. With the nurse right there, they began immediate lifesaving procedures and swiftly rushed him into surgery. By the time I got there, he was already back in his room in ICU.

For four-and-a-half weeks, Dad was in ICU under a drug-induced coma. It was heart-rending to look at him. The once athletic body which had already been affected by age and weight gain now lay prostrate on the bed with more tubes and lines running out of him than I would have thought possible. It was incredibly painful to see him in this condition.

Those weeks took on a nightmarish blur, as life assumed a horrific routine. I would work during the day, make the hour-long drive to the hospital, visit with a non-responding Dad, take Mom home from the hospital, and stay with her at night. The next morning, I would make the long drive to work, while Johnny would pick Mom up and take her to the hospital. At the end of the work day, the cycle would start all over again. It was a grueling schedule, and often, I would be operating on little sleep.

The staff and the nurses in the ICU were outstanding and genuinely cared about the patients. We spent a lot of time with them and grew to love them for their efforts. There were some doctors, however, who were noted for having a lack of tact.

There was one day at work I got a call from my sister-in-law Judy. Mom was in a panic and was asking for all of the family to come in. I left work and started making the journey down, all the while thinking the worst.

When I arrived and everyone was gathered, we found out what happened. One of those "tactless" doctors had taken it upon himself to advise our elderly mother. He had met with her alone while the rest of the family was at work. He bluntly told her that she needed to take him off of all support, not revive him, and let him die. At his age, he would not have a "quality of life." He tried to imply that this is what Dad would want. (How would he know what Dad would want?)

This threw my eighty-six-year-old Mom into a state of extreme alarm. At this point we were still hoping for a recovery. It was as if the man was pressing her for a decision. She would not make a decision, she said, until she talked with all of the family.

Let me be quick to add that I believe that most doctors care about their patients. But to corner my mother alone and hit her with this was, I felt, more than tactless. It was reprehensible. If a doctor has an unpleasant prospect that he needs to address, he needs to do it with the entire family present, so that they can talk it out. On top of that, he made it sound like because of Dad's age, he wasn't worth saving.

This happened several weeks into the ordeal. By this time, Dad had a few moments where he was coherent. My brother John was able to talk to Dad, and explain that they wanted to try some different things, and asked him if he wanted to be revived if anything went wrong. He replied in the affirmative and said he'd like to stay around a little longer.

We communicated our wishes to the doctor, and it was clear he was not happy with the decision.

There were so many setbacks within the next few weeks. A lung collapsed, he had to be ventilated twice, the possibility of blood clots in his legs, and numerous other things. There was a least twice that I thought we were saying our last farewells to him, but strong-willed Dad would always fight back.

One thing was always an encouragement to us. Even when he was in the coma and we didn't know if he could hear us, when someone would pray with him, he would squeeze their hand.

Slowly Dad began to improve, giving us real hope that he would recover. Coming off of those strong drugs that had kept him in an induced coma left Dad in a confused state of mind. He had no idea what had happened to him. He knew nothing of the cardiac arrest, the collapsed lung, or any of the myriad complications that had occurred. He thought, as he phrased it, "I fell down and got hurt."

He also had no idea how long he had been in ICU. He thought only a couple of days had transpired. When someone mentioned that it had been three or four weeks, he would strongly disagree, saying, "No it hasn't been that long. It's been two days."

As his mind tried to piece together what had happened, I began to realize that because of the drugs, he had been in a dreamlike state. Much of what he said would sound disjointed and nonsensical. He would speak of "riding a bucking bronco," which sounded a lot like the shock from the paddles that restarted his heart.

There were some interesting things he said, however. He still didn't understand the gravity of what had happened to him, but began to say, "I don't know why I fell down and got hurt. But I did get to see *what was behind that wall*." He then began to muse about, "All those people who had also fallen down and gotten hurt."

A little bit of our old Dad began to show through. While one of the nurses was checking on some things, she asked, "Mr. Foster, do you know what I am doing?"

"Yes," he responded. "You're trying to figure out how much money to charge me."

Dad was finally moved out of ICU and into a regular hospital room. He became obsessed with getting out of bed and walking around. All he needed was a little help getting out of the bed. By this time, Dad had been on his back for five or six weeks. He hadn't used his legs at all.

On one particular day, the nurses were going to help him into a wheelchair for a little "outing." They rolled him through the hospital halls to a large window where we could view the backside of Kennesaw Mountain.

As we sat there looking at the scenery, the attendants got him talking about his baseball playing days. They seemed fascinated by his stories of old players he played with, going to spring training with the Cubs, and tales of a long bygone era. It was an enjoyable day, with Dad seeming like his old self again.

When they returned to the room, something happened that was a shock to Dad. They were transferring him to the bed, and one of them lost his grip. Dad went straight to the floor. They finally got him up and back into bed (Dad was a big man). It had an effect on Dad.

A strange look came over him. He asked me, "Did you see that? I fell down and I couldn't get up. There was absolutely no strength in my legs. Nothing but weakness." After such a long time insisting that he could walk around a bit if we would just help him up, it kind of dawned on Dad that he might not walk again.

Dad seemed to be improving and was soon to be released from the hospital. In the meantime, things were not so good at work.

My schedule had left me exhausted, and I was often operating on little sleep. I had missed several days due to our ordeal at the hospital. At least twice we thought that we were saying our final farewells to Dad. The fact that I was taking care of Mom through it all and was often dealing with the doctors had left me emotionally drained. My bosses *did not* understand, and they *did not* care.

I had managed the shipping department there for ten years. Since I felt like I was operating on a diminished capacity, I began temporarily delegating some tasks to those who worked with me. Things were not running as smoothly as they should during that time.

In the middle of everything, they called me in and told me they were demoting me. I would no longer be the manager, and in fact, shipping would operate without a manager (a great business move). Although a few months later they would restore me to the manager position, the damage was already done.

The load I was carrying was tremendous. To do this while I was handling the situation with Dad had a harmful effect on me. My Gethsemane experience was about to take another turn.

They then decided to write me up. It all became too much. I had always been one to keep on working through no matter what was going on in my life. For the first time in my life, I felt like it was more than I could handle. I asked for an unpaid two-week leave of absence. I just could not continue on like that. I needed a break.

To make things just a little worse, when I was asking for the time off, the boss used the opportunity to take a personal shot at me, which was a real classy thing to do.

I decided to use the time to take care of some things for Dad. We had some decisions to make. The hospital was about to release Dad. He still couldn't walk. Because of being ventilated twice, including the time he pulled the tubes out by himself, there had been damage done to the flap in his throat that kept food from going into his lungs. His diet was restricted to soft items. He needed more care while he recuperated.

We still had hopes that he would get back on his feet again. To do this, he needed therapy. This was leading to an unpleasant decision. Dad had long said that he never wanted to be placed in a nursing home. The only place he could receive the therapy he needed to get back on his feet was a home. I began visiting homes, looking at the rehab facilities. Our idea was to place Dad in one only as long as it took to recover so that he could resume a normal existence. In my mind, I thought that if he couldn't recover fully, we would find a way to bring him home and take care of him there.

In retrospect, it was not a very realistic goal.

We found a home that had good rehab facilities and seemed to be staffed with people dedicated to the rehabilitation of its tenants.

The day that Dad was transferred was a very cold day. When I met them, they had transferred him without a blanket. He had been outside for a while, and I found my eighty-five-year-old father shivering uncontrollably. I went in search of some attendants and collected several blankets to wrap around him to warm him up. It was not a good start to his time there.

In spite of my assurances to Dad that he was only here to get him back on his feet through rehabilitation, and that we would not just leave him there, I don't think Dad ever got over the idea that he was in a nursing home. I believe that he began to lose heart over the prospect. Whenever I'd make a statement to the effect that I couldn't wait on him to get back on his feet, a look would come over his face that said, "I'll never walk again."

Dad developed a case of diarrhea that lasted a couple of weeks. We had been assured that he would be checked regularly by a doctor. What that meant was there would be one doctor for the entire place who would show up once a week. So his case went untreated for a while.

Because of his diarrhea, he would have absolutely no energy when they took him to rehab. This caused them to think, as I heard them say, "Mr. Foster only does what he wants to do." I believe he became less than a priority for them.

Things were not progressing well.

Christmas was approaching and our Santa Claus was in a nursing home. I had bought a small Christmas tree to place in his room. I set it up and decorated it to try and bring some cheer into the room. Dad seemed to appreciate it.

The Saturday before Christmas, we celebrated at the rest home with Dad. We received permission to use one of the dining areas for our gathering. We had the whole family show up. Myself, Mom, Johnny's family, grandchildren and their wives, and great-grandchildren were all gathered to spend this time with Dad.

In preparation for this, Dad had made sure that the nurses knew he had to be up, neatly shaved, and ready for the event.

When we were all together and they wheeled him in, it presented an image that remains close to my heart to this day. There was Dad, all dressed up and nice, ready to celebrate another Christmas with his family. Although the physical wear on him was still evident, he looked more like the old Dad than he had in the past nine weeks.

With the great-grandchildren leading the way, we all gave our gifts to him. Then we began to sing Christmas carols. The way Dad watched the great-grandchildren while they sang was particularly moving. Several people commented on it.

Dad had been flat on his back for such a long time that he couldn't even sit up for long periods of time without getting nauseated. He had been sitting quite a while when someone suggested to me that Dad was feeling the effects.

I asked Dad, "Do you want to go back to your room?"

"No," he replied, "I want to stay here." It was clear he was enjoying this time with his family.

After a while longer, he began heaving; almost to the point of throwing up. He'd had all the "good cheer" his body could handle. I went looking for the nurses to help take him back to his room.

I was standing outside the room while the nurses helped him back into bed. I overheard him say to the nurses, "This has been a *great* day!"

Christmas day dawned. After spending some time with the rest of the family, I took Mom to see Dad.

Dad's mood was totally different. He seemed forlorn. We asked him how he was doing. In the saddest voice imaginable, he said, "It's Christmas day, and I haven't bought a single gift for anyone."

It was all about "giving" to Dad, and not having something to give really hurt Dad.

New Year's Eve. December 31, 2011.

I was driving back down to Marietta New Year's Eve morning. I had been trying to get back to sleeping at home and developing some sense of normalcy. For about two months, I had been staying exclusively with Mom. The back and forth had left its mark on me, as, indeed, the entire episode had affected the entire family. I was driving down to visit with Mom and go to see Dad.

I received a call from Mom. "Could you stay the night with me?" she asked. It turns out she had gotten dizzy and fallen. Luckily, she had fallen across the bed, was not hurt, and was able to get up. She was afraid of being alone that night.

Of course, I said, "Sure, I will. I'll have to turn around and get me a change of clothes and an overnight bag for tomorrow."

I was so exhausted, that when I hung up, I thought, *No rest for the weary*. I hate to admit that this crossed my mind, but that was the way the past ten weeks had affected me. I was near the end of my stamina.

But, there's nothing I wouldn't do for Mom, so I turned around and drove back to get the things I would need to stay overnight.

When I finally got all that I needed and headed back down, I received another call from Mom. She had been sick for a while and wasn't feeling well that morning, so I would head to the home first to see Dad, then go by to stay with Mom. Mom had gotten a call from Dad. He seemed disturbed and mentally distraught over a lack of care at the home.

Mom wanted me to have a little talk with Dad. We were still holding out hope for a full recovery, but some disquieting events had occurred recently that left me troubled. While our cousin Brenda Christian and her husband Bobby had been visiting with Dad, they had come to take him to rehab. He had refused to go. Also, a time or two recently when I was talking to Dad over the phone, his speech was beginning to sound a little slurred. Mom was wanting me to emphasize to Dad the importance of the rehab to his recovery.

When I arrived, I could tell that Dad was a little agitated. The longer I visited with him, the better he seemed to be doing.

I looked at Dad. I just couldn't bring myself to "lecture" him. Instead, I decided on something else. I rose, when it was time to go, and stood by his bed.

I began, "Dad, while you were in the hospital, I prayed over you many times. I'd like to do that now."

I began to pray out loud. I prayed for his well-being. I prayed for his peace of mind, and for the Lord's comforting presence in his life. I don't really remember all that I prayed for, but I don't think I mentioned his recovery except in passing.

I believe that the Lord was directing my prayer, for as I prayed, an amazing calm and peace came over Dad. The distress he had been experiencing was gone.

As I turned to go, I asked, "Is there any message you want me to give Mom?"

He said, "Yes. Earlier when I called her I was very disturbed. Tell her I'm all right now."

Later that evening when Mom called him, he sounded much more upbeat.

"I'm eating green beans!" he exulted. "Do you know how long it's been since I ate green beans?" The simplest of things were giving him pleasure.

Even though it was New Year's Eve, I turned in early. I was just too exhausted and didn't feel like celebrating the turn of a new year.

12:10 AM. January 1, 2012.

I jerked awake with a start. It took a second to realize that it was the ringing phone that had disturbed my sleep. Before I could stir from bed, the ringing stopped. Almost immediately, my cell phone went off. Deep inside, I knew, though I didn't want to admit it yet.

It was the home. "Mr. Foster was found unresponsive, and has been rushed to the hospital."

"I'm on my way," I replied.

Mom, who had not gone to bed and was in the next room, called out, "Was that the home?"

I called out, "They've taken Dad to the hospital. We need to get ready and go."

Mom began getting ready, while I called my brother Johnny. They lived closer to the hospital than Mom did and would be the first to arrive.

As we sped over the seemingly deserted roads at the very start of a new year, all sorts of thoughts were running through my mind. Even though I knew, there was a part of me that held out hope. I was remembering all the days in the hospital, the setbacks and the progress. I was thinking of going through that all over again.

Mom was saying, "If he's had another 'incident' he'll never survive this one."

"We don't know that, Mom." I said, but *I knew.*

We arrived at the hospital, and I went in to borrow a wheelchair to take Mom in. We waited at the emergency room desk while they called for someone to come get us. Standing there with Mom, the dread inside of me was growing.

They took us into a room where a doctor was waiting for us. Johnny and Judy were already there. Judy was quietly crying. Johnny came over and put his arm around Mom.

"Is he gone?" Mom asked.

Without saying a word, Johnny nodded and gave Mom a hug.

The doctor, in her most respectful tone, expressed her sympathy, and began to relate to us the series of events and the efforts they had made to try and revive Dad to no avail. I barely heard what she was saying.

Then they took us in to see Dad.

It was the beginning of a new year. It was the beginning of a new era in the life of our family; an era without Dad as the stabilizing rock of our family.

* * * * *

I had mentioned that Dad was the stabilizing rock in our family, but the truth is that there is another, stronger rock to lean on in times of distress. It is the rock that you can base your entire life on. It was the rock upon which Dad had built his life, which was why he could be such a dependable force in our lives. By example and by word, he had shown us that it was the only dependable foundation to build our lives upon.

That rock is the Lord Jesus Christ. There is no more solid place to turn for comfort.

Where can you find a supernatural peace during a time of storm? It is in the one who spoke and calmed the storm.

Where can you find hope in the "valley of the shadow of death?" It is in the one who cried out "Lazarus! Come forth!" and death had to bow to his will.

Where can you turn when your heart is crushed? You turn to the one whose heart was "crushed" in Gethsemane, knowing that he bore that burden for you.

Just as death was not too big an obstacle for the Lord, the load you are bearing is not too big for him. It may seem unique to you, and you feel that surely no one has ever experienced what you are going through. Regardless of the nature of your pain, you can rest assured that Jesus has already experienced it.

All the pain, hurt, and sorrow we experience was wrapped up and laid upon the Lord that night in Gethsemane. Everything we could possibly imagine was shouldered by him in his agony.

He understands *perfectly.*

In fact, he had a unique relationship with death.

Jesus was personally acquainted with death

Jesus had contended with death many times during his time on earth.

There was the time Jesus had chanced upon a funeral procession. They were carrying the young man to his place of burial. Death thought he had a tight grip on his prize. It was a done deal.

Jesus stopped the procession and laid his hand on the bier. It was as if he said to death, "Not so fast there, buddy! I have a say in this matter."

With a word, life came pulsing back into the dead and the living man was restored to his mother.

That must have been a rude awakening to death.

Jesus ran into death again in a *private setting*. A ruler of the synagogue, Jairus by name, had come to Jesus asking him to come to his house to lay hands on and heal his daughter who was grievously ill. Jesus went with him. After some delays while healing some other people, a member of Jairus's household met them with some sad news.

"Your daughter has died. No need to bother the Master any longer."

Jesus reassured him, "Don't fear. Your daughter shall be made well again."

When they arrived, Jesus put all the mourners out, and went in privately with only the parents and a couple of his disciples. There in the privacy of her room, Jesus brushed death aside and said, "Little maid, arise."

At his words, the breath of life surged back through the little girl's body, and she was restored to her parents.

Death must have been fairly seething at that one.

But it was the *very public demonstration* that must have sent death over the edge.

It was at the tomb of Lazarus that Jesus had proclaimed for all to hear:

I am the resurrection, and the life: he that believeth in me, though he were dead, yet shall he live: and whosoever liveth and believeth in me shall never die. Believest thou this?
(Jn 11:25–26, KJV)

Death once again had to step aside as Lazarus came forth out of that cold, dark tomb; a living, breathing person.

Whenever death ran into Jesus, he succumbed to the encounter. But the greatest collision was yet to come.

Jesus stared death in the face in Gethsemane

It was perhaps the greatest stare-down contest in history. Neither side blinked. Head to head, Jesus was facing *his own death*, not that of another.

Death was after its greatest prize; the Son of God himself.

Would death wilt away or claim the spoils?

Would the Son of God flee from the face of death, or rush right toward it?

For a time, it seemed that death had the upper hand, for Jesus did, in fact, die. He was laid low in a grave, while death exulted in its "final" victory. After many setbacks, death must have thought, "I always win out!"

But three days later, the unstoppable power of God surged through that tomb, and death's tenuous grip on the Lord was broken. The unbeatable enemy was defeated. In the end, it proved to be no contest. Jesus was Lord even over death.

Because of what he accomplished, there is a truth we can cling to when we face the "finality" of death.

He gave us Hope beyond the grave

For the Christian, this world is not home. All of our hopes and dreams are centered in another world. That world is our home. When Christ comes into a heart, he implants within that person a hope that transcends this world.

That world is where Christ is. He went before us to prepare a place for us. It is prepared especially for us. With a *new home* and a *new hope*, then death becomes merely the transition to that new home.

Not only did he give us a new home, but he gave us *a new comforter*. He sent us the Holy Spirit to work within our hearts during times of grief.

He DOES NOT TAKE DEATH AWAY, but he does remove the "sting" of death. He does not take "grief" away, but brings comfort in the midst of grief.

The grieving process is natural and necessary for our well-being. You could no more remove the grieving process than you could remove death. It is coming for all of us, but we don't have to be "overcome" by grief.

What he *does* do is something supernatural. He gives us a *supernatural strength to stand.* As a child of his, we find that we can bear what we did not think was possible to bear. We find a calm and peace that we did not know existed. Our grief is turned into an expectation that one day we will be re-united with our loved ones in the presence of Christ. What a joyful day that will be!

I could not leave this thought without stating that this promise of peace is predicated on being one of his. If I have a relationship with God, then I have this promise of peace.

That relationship is found in the one who knelt in Gethsemane; the one who bore all of our sorrows and pain for us.

In Christ alone is my hope found.

In Christ alone can I have victory over death.

In Christ alone can I face the testing of sorrow.

CHAPTER 9

The Call for Service

"By any chance, are you related to Preacher Ralph Foster?"

I don't know how many times I've been asked that question. When someone finds out I'm a preacher and that my last name is Foster, that question is likely to be posed to me. I'm always proud to respond, "Yes, he was my granddaddy."

Granddaddy was a country Baptist preacher who preached with a lot of fire. He pastored several small churches in North Georgia and had a regular radio broadcast at eight thirty every Sunday morning on WFOM radio in Marietta, Georgia. He was on the radio for over twenty years.

Granddaddy was of the "shoe-squeaking" variety of preacher. Let me explain what I mean by that.

Bro. Jack Cole, an outstanding preacher, shared with me a story about my granddaddy that I found amusing. It occurred during the time Bro. Jack was wrestling with the call to preach. He was directing the choir at a particular church and Granddaddy had come to preach a revival. Jack was sitting on the platform while Granddaddy was preaching.

This was in the days before churches were air-conditioned. Instead every pew had a fan, adorned with advertisement from the local funeral home, in the rack beside the hymnal. While the preacher was preaching, everybody in the congregation would be furiously fanning themselves trying to keep cool.

Granddaddy would preach with such a fire that the sweat would run down him under his suit and collect in his shoes. Jack said that when he would walk across the pulpit area, his shoes would squeak.

After Granddaddy finished preaching, Jack got up and said to the congregation, "I don't know if God is calling me to preach or not, but if he does, I want to be one of those 'shoe-squeaking' preachers."

When I said he preached with "fire," I meant that there was a real passion in his preaching. This was really brought home to me by a funny little incident that happened to me once.

I had just started preaching and was in my twenties when I was asked to go preach at a particular church. It just so happened that Granddaddy had preached there the Sunday before I did.

Prior to the service, I was sitting on the front row. There were a couple of precious, sweet, older ladies sitting right behind me. Before the service even started these sweet ladies were praying out loud, "Lord, bless today. Be with the preacher today."

That really grabbed my attention! I was thinking to myself, *Bless God! We're really going to have a meeting today!*

All during the song service, these precious sweet ladies continued to pray, "Lord, fill the preacher with the Spirit."

I was really getting fired up by that time. When it was finally my turn, I really cut loose. From the first word, I really had liberty. I hit the ground wide open to choruses of "Amen!" with these precious and sweet ladies right in the middle of them.

What a time we had! God really blessed in that service.

Afterward, I was standing in the back of the church greeting people, and I noticed those precious and sweet ladies waiting in line to greet me.

I hate to admit that my mind was working this way, but they had enjoyed the service so much I was preparing myself to "graciously" accept any compliment they bestowed upon me.

When they finally reached me, they looked me up and down, and the first one said, "Well, you're all right, I reckon, but we like your granddaddy much better."

It was then that I realized that my granddaddy was a hard act to follow. (By the way, you will never offend me by bragging on my granddaddy.)

I remember all the stories that he shared with us; how he got saved at home behind the barn during revival meetings. About the great revival that broke out at Olive Springs Baptist Church, where my parents, aunt and uncle, and a host of others came to the Lord. All those stories are precious in my memory.

The truth is Granddaddy surrendered to the call to preach rather late in life. He was approximately forty years of age, and preached on till his death at the age of eighty-eight.

Granddaddy owned a small store in the old Fair Oaks Community of Marietta, Georgia. It sat on the opposite corner from Floyd's Barber Shop (sounds like something from the *Andy Griffith Show*, doesn't it?) He concerned himself with making a living and providing for his family, like any good man would.

Granddaddy had to have a Gethsemane experience to bring him to the point of surrender to God's will. In his case, it struck his only son, my dad, when he was a senior in high school.

Dad fell sick and was bedridden, at the point of death, nearly his entire high school year. From the vantage point of over seventy years later, the illness takes on something of a mystery. I'm not sure I can tell you what the illness was. I'm not sure they ever identified it.

Granddaddy finally told God that he would preach the gospel for him.

The story of Granddaddy's first sermon is amazing to me.

On his way to his first sermon, Granddaddy had not even told my grandmother, Flossie, that he had been called to preach. He told her he was just going to give a "little talk" to them at the church. When they got to the church, Granddaddy told Flossie to go on in and find a seat, and he would be in directly.

While Flossie found a seat, Granddaddy went around behind the church to pray.

Several people seated around Flossie were telling her how excited they were to hear Granddaddy's first sermon, to which Flossie replied, "Oh no. He's just going to give a 'little talk.'"

The service started with some of that great singing those old churches were known for, and Granddaddy still hadn't shown up.

In the meantime, Granddaddy was really wrestling with it. Fear began to overtake him. He finally concluded, "I can't do this. I just don't have the ability."

With fear getting the better part of him, he thought, *I'll just go up on the church steps, get Flossie's attention, and go home. I just can't do this!*

Granddaddy walked up on the steps and stopped. The congregation was singing:

> Rock of Ages, Cleft for me,
> *Let me hide myself in thee.*

At that moment, the Spirit of God came flooding over Granddaddy. The fear fled away. He walked straight up to the pulpit and began to preach. He preached with the same power, zeal, and passion that he would become known for over the years. God moved in a miraculous way in that service.

His first sermon lasted about an hour.

Though starting late in life with only a seventh-grade education, he preached for forty-eight years and made a strong impact on his corner of the world, and left a lasting legacy behind him.

* * * * *

Serving the lord Jesus Christ is the greatest joy that there is. Wait a second, let me rephrase that. It is the second greatest joy. The absolute greatest is when the Lord Jesus came into my heart and saved me. Knowing that my sins are forgiven, and that I have an ongoing, growing relationship with him outpaces by far any other joy.

Outside of that, nothing compares to doing what you are "called" to do. That considered, it makes me wonder why so many of us, myself included, are hesitant to yield to that calling.

Most people, when they refer to their calling, they are refer-ring to what they *want* to do with their life. That's not an accurate description of what a calling is.

In its simplest form, this could be a definition of what "calling" means: *Our calling is God's plan for our lives.* That may seem like a small distinction to you, but it is a vitally important one. It brings us to our first conclusion.

Our Calling is not of our own choosing

I have had people ask me before, "How did you choose to become a preacher?" I didn't. It was God's choice. He laid the path for me. I merely had to find that path that he had marked out for my life.

The Prophet Jeremiah was fully cognizant of that fact. He records in the book of Jeremiah:

> **Then the word of the Lord came unto me, say-ing, Before I formed thee in the belly, I knew thee; and before thou camest out of the womb I sanctified thee, and I ordained thee a prophet unto the nations.** (Jer. 1:4–5, KJV)

He recognized that there was a holy, divine plan for his life. It originated in the very heart of God. God's plan was reliant upon the fact that *God knew Jeremiah personally and intimately.* He made him; knew his personality with all of its quirks; and designed the path he would walk.

The same could be said for us. God made us and knows our inner workings. He has laid out a plan for our lives that will lead to a life of service and fulfillment.

Before I surrendered to the call to preach, I had my life all planned out. I knew what I wanted to do. I wanted to be a gospel singer, which wasn't too realistic when you consider I had an average voice at best.

I jokingly tell people that at one time, I thought I was called into the music ministry. Then the Lord *heard* me sing and decided he better find something else for me to do.

I had taken piano lessons but they just didn't "take" with me. I learned just enough to be able to arrange four-part vocals, and actually served as music director of a couple of churches.

But what I really wanted to do was to sing bass for a gospel quartet. I have always loved quartet music. When I finally realized that my voice wasn't really low enough to be a good bass, I decided I could be a baritone.

In spite of my limited abilities, my desire remained to perform on stage, singing those gospel songs I so loved.

My thinking got turned upside down when I was twenty-two years of age. I was a member of Shiloh Hills Baptist Church and was working along with some other people in the youth department. A spirit of revival broke out among the youth and we began seeing God move in wondrous ways.

It was after one of our Tuesday night youth meetings when a group of us were standing around talking. One of the young girls in the group came flying back into the parking lot in her car, hopped out in tears, and said to all of us standing there, "I need you to help me pray. I want to know what God's will for me is. Does he want me to go to the mission field?"

We all went back inside, gathered around her in the altar, and began to intercede. Every time I tried to lift her need up, I found it difficult to pray for her. It was as it the Lord was saying, "You are trying to pray for her, but *you need to pray for yourself.* There is something that I am wanting *you* to do."

For the first time, it was beginning to dawn on me that what I wanted the Lord's will to be might not actually *be* His will. He was starting to implant within me a new vision, a new burden, and a new desire. The best I can describe what I was beginning to envision is this: I longed to see people coming to the Lord Jesus; yearning to get their sin-burden lifted. I just wanted to be the sign post, pointing to the cross.

The word I was getting from the Lord was, "PREACH THE GOSPEL!"

But, it was hard to give up the old desire. For five days, I struggled with it. I was enrolled at Georgia State University studying business at the time. I would be sitting in marketing class, which is hardly a spiritual setting, and the burden and conviction would sweep over me. I couldn't even pay attention in class. There was that all-consuming burden pounding away in my chest: PREACH THE GOSPEL! PREACH THE GOSPEL! PREACH THE GOSPEL!

It all came to a head that next Sunday night. The burden was heavy upon me. All during the service, I could think of one thing. The invitation came and went. I did not move.

As they were praying the benediction, I was standing there next to a friend of mine, Phil Brownlee. *What I'll do,* I thought to myself, *Is just ask Phil to pray for me.*

With the "Amen," I motioned for Phil to follow me, and we stepped into a room off of the main sanctuary. What I was going to say was, "Phil, I want you to pray for me. I *think* I *might* be called to preach."

When I opened my mouth, I just broke down in tears, and what came out was, "Phil, I'm CALLED TO PREACH!"

Phil ran and got our pastor, Dr. Tolbert Moore. He came in, and, after some serious praying, he asked a straightforward question. "Has God given you the desire to preach? Do you want to preach?"

My response was, "You don't know how much I want to."

We walked back out to the platform. Most of the church was still there. Shiloh Hills Baptist had a habit of fellowshipping long after the service was ended. Preacher Moore got everyone's attention, and said simply, "Listen to this."

To the best of my recollection, I said, "All this time, I thought I was called into music, but tonight I'm letting you know that I'm *called to preach*!!"

Oh, what rejoicing! People lined up to hug my neck and to pledge their prayers for me. Some seemed surprised. Some actually said, "We already knew." But what it took was my being willing to do whatever God desired.

I was in such a hurry to get out and tell someone that I didn't know what else was going on. As I was walking out of the building, I noticed that Dr. Moore's son and one of my friends, Gary Moore, was praying with some people. I didn't know till a few days later that, after I left, the burden fell on Gary, and he confessed his calling to preach. A lot can happen after a service is ended.

When I called Granddaddy and told him I had surrendered to the call to preach, without even pausing to think, he said, "You're preaching for me next Sunday night." He firmly believed that the best thing for a young preacher was to get him preaching immediately.

And so it was, that one week after confessing the call, I preached my first sermon.

The point to be taken here is that in order to come to the point of total surrender, I had to give up my own plans for my life.

Because of that

Surrendering to the call can take on a Gethsemane feel

It's not easy *giving up your dreams and desires*. They are too ingrained within our being. That is why many Christians put up barriers and say, "I'll only grow this far. Only enough Jesus to give me a home in heaven and make me feel good! But I just can't be totally committed!"

No Christian would actually *say* those words. They know better. But deep inside, that is what is driving them. Even though they surrendered to Christ as Lord when they were saved, they still have a tendency to wrestle control of their lives away. They want to be master of their own destiny.

Just like Christ in Gethsemane, they must come *face to face with death*. Specifically, they must put their own desires to death. Your love for the Lord Jesus must take absolute priority in your life.

You have to come to the place where you say, Like Jesus did, "NEVERTHELESS NOT MY WILL, BUT THINE BE DONE!" A whole new world will then open up for you. The avenues for service to the Lord are innumerable. Not everyone will be a preacher like I am. But you will find your place of service within the body of Christ.

Once I finally surrendered, I discovered something.

There is joy in surrendering

To put things in southern vernacular, my "want to" changed. No longer was I satisfied to immerse myself in music. Now I had an overwhelming desire to proclaim this wonderful message. If I'm not doing it, I'm a restless soul indeed.

Not everyone is going to be called to preach, or as I sometimes refer to it, to "rip and roar." Thank God for those who are genuinely called into the music ministry. What a blessing they are. Our lives would be a little less bright without them. And I am truly amazed at those talented individuals, my brother John being one of them, who have been able to combine the callings of pastor-preacher and music at the same time. But that is not my calling.

The point is, this is where I find my joy. It is in serving the Lord Jesus Christ in the calling *he chose for me.*

Let me make a few observations concerning his call.

When we feel like our abilities are insufficient to do what he calls us to do, *he enables us* to do the task.

I'm amazed at how many times in scripture the person called felt inadequate. Gideon said, "Lord, I'm from a small family and I'm the least in my family."

Moses said, "I'm of slow speech. How can I speak to Pharaoh?"

Isaiah, when he saw the Lord high and lifted up, uttered, "Woe is me. I am unclean, and I'm of a people with unclean lips."

Over and over, when faced with the Lord's greatness and over-whelmed by the magnitude of the task, these great men of God begged off thinking they were not up to the challenge. Over and over, God proved that he could take a weak vessel and do a great work through that vessel. Whatever the objection, God showed that he was more than adequate to overcome that shortcoming.

In fact, when God takes a frail human and does something miraculous, Jesus Christ is glorified! All credit has to go to him, because it for sure wasn't the frail human who did it.

The second thing I'd like to notice, is that when we surrender to his will, *it becomes our passion!* When God lays a burden on your heart and you respond to it, an amazing thing happens. It is turned into a passion.

Sometimes I wonder if we haven't become a little too clinical in the church today when we approach the idea of finding our calling. They may say, "Find your spiritual gift, and that will be your calling." They may even resort to taking a "spiritual gifts test."

Don't get me wrong. I believe in spiritual gifts. Anyone who believes the Bible does. I've even taken the spiritual gift test. It is interesting to take, and in my case, turned out to be very accurate.

But why would we want to take such an approach? I find it preferable to cry out to God, "Lord, what will you have me do?" When my heart has wrestled with the Lord, like Jacob did, and settled beyond doubt what God's will for my life is, then *that is where the passion comes from.*

Lord, deliver us from dry-eyed, clinical ministries. We have enough of them. Instead we need heart-stirring, impassioned Men of God who have a burden for the work. Someone who has been through Gethsemane, and is willing to give of himself totally to the cause of Christ.

Finally, being obedient to God's will for my life has brought a high level of *fulfillment and satisfaction* to my life. It is a satisfaction that is not dependent upon someone else's idea of what constitutes success. I have not "arrived." I am still striving to attain the next goal; the next plateau. And it is in that striving that I find my fulfillment.

For you see, I am doing what HE set me aside to do. And I will continue to do it. And I hope I am still learning, growing, and striving till the day I go home to glory.

That is why I say that the greatest joy in life, outside of being saved, is in serving the Lord Jesus Christ. You never know what lies ahead. There's always another adventure around the bend.

Most of what I have said concerning a "calling" might sound like I'm referring strictly to the call to preach, for that is what I have personally experienced. But not everyone is called to preach. Many are called into a ministry of music, called to teach a Sunday school class, called to work with youth, or any number of other areas of service.

All of them carry the same importance in the life of the church. All of them bring the same satisfaction. All of them are faced with the same challenges and setbacks. All of them bring the same reward.

It is the most beautiful of things, when a body of believers have found their place of service, and work together as a well-oiled machine serving the Lord Jesus.

What better cause is there than to lift up the one who knelt in Gethsemane.

For this cause we also, since the day we heard of it, do not cease to pray for you, and to desire that ye might be filled with the knowledge of his will in all wisdom and spiritual understanding;

That ye might walk worthy of the Lord unto all pleasing, being fruitful in every good work, and increasing in the knowledge of God;

Strengthened with all might, according to his glorious power, unto all patience and long-suffering with joyfulness;

Giving thanks unto the Father, which hath made us meet to be partakers of the inheritance of the saints in Light. (Col. 1:9–12, KJV)

CHAPTER 10

The Call for Salvation

"I checked into the hotel with a bottle of whiskey and a gun. My intentions were to finish off the whiskey, and then finish off myself. God intended something else for my life that night."

I have always enjoyed an old-fashioned testimony meeting. You don't see too many of them anymore, but in my youth, there were many times they proved to be a blessing.

It might begin when an old saint of God would stand with tears in their eyes and share with the congregation a recent blessing from God. Then, one by one, people would get up and begin sharing the goodness of God. They might tell of their salvation experience, or about a recent encounter with God. It was always good to hear how a person had come to the Lord, or what was going on in a person's life. Many a good "sermon" was preached by those testimonies.

They were never planned. Some things you just can't plan for. In those services, there was a freedom to testify as the Spirit compelled you to. That was the key; as the Spirit moved. I have seen people come to the Lord, and wayward Christians repent at some of those meetings.

Although I believe everything should be done decently and in order, and that a change in the service should only happen if the Spirit leads, a part of me misses the freedom of those days.

It was at one of those meeting when I was a teenager, that I heard one of the most moving testimonies of salvation that I had ever heard. It has stuck with me close to fifty years.

To the best of my recollection, the following account is an accurate rendition of that testimony. Please forgive me if my "fuzzy" memory gets some of the details wrong, but the gist of the story is true. This is the testimony as I remember it.

Jon (a fictitious name) was an "up and comer" in the business world. With a young wife and starting a new family, the future seemed bright for him.

It all started with an occasional drink at social gatherings connected to work. Jon was about to fall prey to the fiction that he could drink in moderation and that he could control his consumption. He rationalized it by saying to himself that it was necessary to socialize this way to advance in the business world.

Before long, he was having a drink at home to "unwind" and relax. Unknown to Jon, something deep inside of him was beginning to develop a dependence on that drink. He never saw what was happening or what was about to happen. How could he have?

It got to the point where he needed a little something during the day while at work. He would spike his cup of coffee at work from a small flask he kept hidden. He thought he was hiding it well, but everybody knew what was going on.

His work began to suffer. His evaluation reviews began to reflect this. Where once he had gotten praise and high marks, he was getting dismal reports with remarks like "attitude needs to improve."

He was finally called into the office and was given a written reprimand. Along with the written word, he was given a verbal ultimatum, "Either you straighten out what's going on, or you're out of here! TERMINATED!"

Meanwhile, things at home were going from bad to worse to, "Oh my goodness, What now!" The arguments with his wife escalated, getting more vicious with each passing day. Finally, the unthinkable happened; something he never would have done. In a drunken fit, he slapped his wife; HARD! She fell to the ground. Jon could not believe the look she gave him. There was *fear* painted on her face. *Fear of him!* He would have given anything to take back that slap, but it was too late.

She bundled up her kids and escaped to safety that night.

Meanwhile, the worst happened at work. He was unceremoniously cut loose. The job market being what it was, there wasn't much available for someone who had been terminated. Add to the fact that Jon had lost all drive and desire and his days had become a mere existence.

With his house teetering on foreclosure, the possibility of permanently losing his family, and nothing of value to cling to, it seemed to Jon that life just was not worth living any longer.

It was time to end it.

He checked into the hotel room, and carried in two items: a bottle of whiskey and a gun. It only seemed appropriate to him that with so much of his life given over to drink, his last action on earth would be to indulge this weakness one more time.

He set the bottle and the gun down side by side on the desk and sat down looking at them. He didn't know what prompted him to do it, but he slid open the drawer.

There, staring him in the face, was a Gideon Bible that had been left open by someone. Jon looked closely and saw that there was a passage underlined.

I am the door: by me if any man enter in, he shall be saved, and shall go in and out and find pasture. The thief cometh not, but for to kill, and to destroy: I am come that they might have life, and that they might have it more abundantly. I am the good shepherd: the good shepherd giveth his life for the sheep. (Jn 10:9–11, KJV)

Jon picked up the Bible, holding it in his left hand. His right hand reached out and gripped the gun. He sat there gazing at the two as if he were weighing both of them. One hand was offering him life. The other promised death.

Memories began flooding through his mind as he sat there; childhood memories of attending a small church with his parents who had passed away too early. He was trying to remember anything the preacher had said, but couldn't bring to mind a single word. It was more a feeling that was stirring within him. A feeling that there was just something missing.

Then things started popping one after another into his mind. Different people who had spoken to him about how this person, Jesus Christ, had changed their life. He had dismissed it all at the time as just more religious talk. It hadn't had an effect on him at the time, but now each word began surging into his conscientiousness and wouldn't seem to let go.

He set the gun down, turned his attention to the Bible, and began reading more.

Early into the morning he read. Each new page brought an awareness to him that there had always been a huge hole in his life. Even when things had been good, it had been there nagging him.

Finally, at the end of his senses, He got out of the chair and knelt down by the bed. He spread the Bible out before him and began to pray the only way he knew how.

"Lord, I've made a mess of my life. I've hurt everyone I've ever loved. I'm sorry for the way I've lived my life. I don't know how, but is there any way you can help me?" And as he broke down in tears, "Can you forgive me?"

It was almost instantaneous. It was as if a heavy weight had been lifted off him. The despair was replaced by something he couldn't quite describe. Could it be the realization that somebody actually loved him? Could it be the beginnings of joy?

He stood up and realized that things were different. There was no more thought of ending it all, but of *beginning* something.

It might take some time to put everything back together. It might be a long road, but he felt like he was starting a *new life*.

* * * * *

Over the years, I have heard hundreds of personal testimonies of how a person came to Christ. Each one is different and has its own personal appeal. The person who gave this testimony passed away years ago, so I was not able to check the details of it, which is why I used a fictitious name. I may have even gotten a few of the details of another testimony confused with this one. But the basic elements of the story (the intention to commit suicide, the whiskey and the gun, the Gideon bible) are all an accurate depiction of that testimony.

Very few testimonies are as dramatic as this one. For example, I came to Christ as a ten-year-old boy. There wasn't a whole lot of opportunities for me to drift into that level of sin. But to me, what happened was every bit as dramatic as that testimony. The meaning it holds for me is every bit as real as the "spectacular" story.

All of the stories have at least two things in common.

First, every person had a *need for a savior*. Whether in deep sin, or if one was considered a "good boy," they came to a realization that there was something that they just could not accomplish on their own.

The second thing they all have in common is that there was a *definite change in the person* after they met Jesus Christ. No one could come face to face with the Lord and remain the same.

Let's take a closer look at these two things.

The need for a Savior is universal

The truth of the matter is that not everyone is going to heaven. It is a prepared home; prepared by the hand of God for those who have received his gift of eternal life. Until a person has received this gift through Jesus Christ, then heaven is not their home.

This is out of sorts with the popular idea that everyone is destined to go to heaven. That is reminiscent of Universalist theology. A Universalist believes that everyone is going to heaven. Even the person who rejects Jesus Christ will supposedly get a second chance after death. Nothing could be farther from the truth.

Universalism is a dangerous theology, giving false hope to thousands of people.

Most of the people who hold to this notion, would not even know what universalism is. They proceed from the notion that if anybody is going to heaven, then certainly I am. Certainly, God must think as I do. There is nothing wrong with me. *I am not a sinner.* I must be going to heaven.

The *only* thing that is universal is our need for a savior. We are all in the same boat. Before Christ came into my heart, I, too, was lost. I had no spiritual life. I needed Jesus to infuse me with his spirit, making me his child.

The reason we need a savior is because of our sin. That's a word people don't like to talk about much anymore. We are all sinners and that is what separates us from God. To have a relationship with God, that question of sin must be dealt with.

But people might object, "God certainly must accept me for who I am. Right?" It is true that a person can come to God as he is and God will accept him, but GOD DOES NOT ACCEPT YOUR SIN. To come to him, God requires *repentance.*

To repent means to *turn away from your sin* and then to turn toward and embrace the Lord Jesus. It means putting away your sin. You could no more come to Christ and still cling to your sin than you could gorge yourself on candy and a lot of sweets without worrying about gaining weight. But people seem to want to claim the parts of God's Word that are attractive to them, but ignore the parts that make them uncomfortable.

But getting someone to acknowledge, or even to see their need is a whole different ball game. When you are committed to the idea that you are all right, it is not easy to change your thinking. And the fact that not many people will admit that they are a sinner makes it that much more difficult.

To get someone to change their entire way of thinking requires divine intervention. I don't have the ability to change a person's heart and mind. No powers of persuasion ever could. To change someone from the inside out, God has to step in.

It is called Holy Spirit conviction. God's Spirit is the agent that convicts a person in their own eyes that they are a sinner. The Spirit *convinces* them of the fact, and begins to draw them to God's point of view.

What follows could be described as a period of near "mourning" as the sinner is confronted with his own failings. It becomes a true Gethsemane experience, for the sinner's eternal destiny hangs in the balance.

It is a time when the soul can experience absolute desolation, but it is the one example we have used where there is instantaneous relief. The instant the sinner repents and calls out to God, the burden is immediately lifted. In its place, the new believer is infused with an overwhelming joy.

That moment when they realize that their sins have been forgiven, they just begin to appreciate the full extent of God's love.

That brings us to the second common denominator in all of these stories.

The difference Jesus makes in a life

My life has not been the same since Jesus Christ came into my heart. That one single event has done more to alter the direction of my life than any other incident. The fact that my entire life has been given to serve the Lord and preach his gospel attests to that fact.

Beyond me, there are untold thousands who could testify to the same thing. In fact, through the centuries, that figure could number in the millions.

There is no better illustration than to go to a passage of scripture written by a man who called himself the "chiefest of sinners." The Apostle Paul described the difference this way:

> Therefor being justified by faith, we have peace with God through our Lord Jesus Christ: by whom also we have access by faith into this grace wherein we stand.
>
> And not only so, but we glory in tribulations also; knowing that tribulation worketh patience; and patience, experience; and experience, hope: and hope maketh not ashamed; because the love of God is shed abroad in our hearts by the Holy Ghost which is given to us.
>
> For when we were yet without strength, in due time Christ died for the ungodly. For scarcely for a righteous man will one die: yet peradventure for a good man some would even dare to die. But God commendeth his love toward us, in that while we were yet sinners, Christ died for us.
>
> Much more then, being now justified by his blood, we shall be saved from wrath through him. (Rom. 5:1–9, KJV)

This passage reveals at least five ways in which Jesus makes a difference in a person's life.

The first difference Jesus makes is *we have a new standing before God.* Verse 1 says we are "justified by faith." At one time, I was a sinner with no standing before God. I had no relationship with him; just a surface knowledge of him.

But when Jesus came into my heart, all of that changed. Now when I approach God, I am not treated as a sinner. He views me as a saint. Better than that, I am his child. It is as if all my sins had *never happened.* That is what it means to be justified. In God's eyes, I have been justified, and he views me as righteous.

Let me be quick to add, it is not my own righteousness. He cloaks me in the righteousness of his son. When he views me, it is through the prism of his son. What he sees is a righteous man, for I am "clothed" in Christ. That is my new standing before God.

I gain access to this position by *grace* through *faith*. Grace can be described as a "gift that has been given to me, which I did not earn." I also did not deserve it, but it has been given to me.

I received this gift through faith. I did not work for it. It was a gift. This gift is described best in the book of Ephesians:

For by grace are ye saved through faith; and that not of yourselves: it is the gift of God: Not of works, lest any man should boast. (Eph. 2:8–9, KJV)

The Apostle Paul then gives us the second way we are different. *We experience his peace.*

If I can let me draw a sketch of life before Jesus came in.

Life has had an unsettled feel about it. Something deep within has seemed incomplete. What I did not realize at the time and certainly would never admit, is that I have been at odds with God. It's like there has been an internal warfare going on. God on the one hand reaching out trying to draw me. I, on the other hand, resisting with all of my might. In my mind, I refuse to admit that I need Jesus, but relentlessly, I am being pursued by the long arm of love.

It truly was WARFARE! I was in opposition to what God was saying to me.

But an amazing thing happened when I surrendered to him. The conflict between God and I came to an end. In its place, there was an enduring calm that invaded my life. This is peace WITH God. No more conflict.

But I also found that I could experience the peace OF God. This is a supernatural peace that envelopes me regardless of what is going on in my world. No matter what storm may be raging, there can be a calm that rules the heart of a believer. It is based in a confidence that I have a loving God who is taking care of me, and I trust him implicitly.

That is the twofold peace we find when Jesus comes into our heart.

The third difference we see in a life given to the Lord is that *we have a new outlook on life*. We view the trials and tribulations that we all experience differently. Instead of dwelling on the negative aspect, we look to see the hand of God at work in our lives. As a Christian grows and matures in grace, he can even reach the point where he rejoices in what the Lord is accomplishing through these events.

The Apostle Paul illustrates this when he outlines a natural progression through trials. The first step in this sequence is that tribulations develop patience. Patience is the ability to approach a difficult situation with a calm spirit as opposed to totally "losing" it. We would never need patience if there were no trials. The way patience is developed is by actually walking through the fire.

Through that God-given patience, we gain experience. When we, by our experience, see that the Lord has been faithful and that he is working in our lives, then our hope grows brighter. Nothing strengthens this confidence like understanding that Jesus has walked every step with you. Not only that, but he understands. He has already been to Gethsemane. He knows.

It really takes a work of grace in a person's life to view things in this manner. It takes a divine touch. It takes God working in our lives, changing us, and making us different.

The fourth difference he outlines is that *we have a new love*. Implanted within the believer is a new type of love; a different type of love. It is a love patterned after the love of God.

It is easy to love those that love us. It is easy to love the beautiful people. It is not so easy to love those who treat us horrendously. How about those who have no "lovely" traits about themselves? How about truly bad or "evil" people? It is hard enough to love someone who is a stranger, or is simply "different" than us.

The love of God is described in this passage as much different. God demonstrated his love toward us in that *while we were still sinners* Jesus died for us. He did not wait for us to reform or get better.

He did not wait for us to love him first. He did not wait for us to deserve or earn that love.

While we were still rejecting him, he loved us.

While we were obnoxious, he loved us.

While we hated the things of God, he loved us.

WHEN WE DID NOT DESERVE IT, he actually gave his life for us.

This is the unconditional love that has been implanted within us. The person who truly believes, realizes where God's love found them. That love will naturally flow from out of his very being. I don't know who originally said this, but I have heard it said, "If you are a Christian, then love ain't an option!"

That's why if you see someone who claims to be a Christian, yet he shows no love, then something is seriously wrong with his relationship. Either he has drifted so far from the Lord that his heart is cold, or he has never really met the Lord.

This does not mean that if you love someone, you have to accept the sin in their life. You can love the person, but you can hate the "cancer" within them. You loathe that thing that is killing and destroying that person.

It is the same way with sin. That sin is destroying that person. It is standing between them and a right relationship with their Creator. You do not accept that. It is your LOVE that causes you to LOATHE what sin is doing to that person.

The love of Christ did something about it. He took that sin upon himself, died for it, rose again, and now offers us the gift of forgiveness.

That is the type of love that has been implanted within us.

The final difference we notice in this passage is that *the judgment of God is no longer upon us.* It was that sin we talked about that separated us from God. It was that sin that lashed out at the heart of God. The very nature of sin is that it is destructive. It tears apart all that it touches. It is the one great obstacle to having a rewarding and fulfilling relationship with God.

The most solemn effect that sin has on a person is that it brings God's judgement upon them. You may say, "I know that one day, there will be a judgement, but I have time."

The fact is, that judgement is already upon you. Just two verses after the wonderful grace verse, John 3:16, the Word of God says this:

He that believeth on him is not condemned: but he that believeth not is condemned already, for he has not believed in the name of the only begotten Son of God. (Jn 3:18, KJV)

Here is the sinner: going about his business, oblivious to the fact that his rejection of a holy God has left God's judgement hanging over his head. It is only God's long-suffering nature that spares him from immediate retribution.

But the good news is found in the first part of John 3:18; "He that believeth on him is not condemned." The moment we come to Christ, that judgment is lifted off of us. We are no longer subject to that judgment. We have been *saved from God's wrath.*

Jesus bore that judgment for us on the cross.

* * * * *

This is why we say that our need for a savior is universal. We all face that same dilemma. The purest saint was a sinner who needed Jesus.

When the call for salvation comes knocking at our door, there may be a period where we wrestle through a Gethsemane experience.

But, oh, the joy when Jesus comes into our heart, bringing forgiveness and taking away our guilt. Gone also will be the grief that accompanied our sin.

God's judgment is lifted!

No longer viewed as a sinner, I am now a child of God!

Oh, happy day!

CHAPTER 11

The Path Out of the Garden

He was exhausted. The night's sleep, which had been nearly nonexistent, had done little to alleviate the turmoil in his mind.

In the faint light of the early morning, John and Peter trudged along, making their way toward the place where they had laid the Master. The toll that the last couple of days had exacted from the two was evident in the way they walked heads down, shoulders hunched, despair seeping out of every pore of their face.

John's mind couldn't help dwelling on the events following Gethsemane. He had turned back and followed at a distance as the guards took Jesus up the path that led out of the garden. As foreboding as Gethsemane was, things did not improve any on that path.

It had been a long night. They had arrived at Caiaphas's house, where there had been a lengthy examination by the high priest. It had been evident by their manner and tone that the outcome was a settled deal. They then took Jesus away to holding while they had conferred among themselves about the best course of action.

Somewhere along the line Peter had shown up, and John had let him into the house. For some reason, Peter had disappeared unexpectedly. John looked over at Peter as they walked. There seemed to be an additional weight bearing down on him, and John didn't feel quite at ease to ask him what had happened.

Beside that John had enough on his mind, as he replayed over and over again those events. There had been the shuffling back and forth between Pilate and Herod, as if neither man wanted his name attached to this problem. It was turning out to be much too thorny a situation.

After it had landed back in Pilate's hands, there was a period of time when Jesus had been removed from their sight. When he reappeared, John was shocked at what he saw.

The bloody spectacle that stood before them hardly resembled a human being any longer. It was not shocking that there had been a scourging. That was a way too common practice with the Romans. But the ferocity of it was jarring to the senses. John was not the squeamish type, but the sight caused his stomach to roll, the nausea rising toward his nose, and he thought he might throw up.

He looked over at Mary, Jesus's mother. Throughout the night, he had been close to her side, trying to offer comfort. But there could be no comfort for her now, as she beheld the soul-crushing image that was her son.

John resisted the urge to be sick, placing his arm around Mary and holding her close.

The memory of it even now brought a wave of nausea down in the pit of his stomach. It was hard to imagine that such barbarity could be inflicted by one human being upon another.

But that was not the worst of it. The heartache that followed next carried the ring of finality with it. It was the ultimate fear. DEATH!

Mary had fairly shuddered in John's arms as they took him to the place of execution. Her whole body would jump with each strike of the hammer. As devastated as John was, he could not imagine what was going on in the heart of Mary.

They stayed till the bitter end. They had experienced everything sorrow could heap upon them. They had dutifully watched as Joseph and Nicodemus had claimed the body, wrapped it, and hastily placed it in Joseph's own tomb because of the approach of Passover. There had been no time to anoint the body.

That's what had led to today's pilgrimage. Some of the women had wanted to anoint the body now that the Passover was concluded.

They would need help with the stone in order to do it. John and Peter had volunteered.

He wasn't looking forward to it. Each step caused his heavy heart to sink a little lower.

As they came around one bend, John was surprised to see Mary Magdalene running toward them. She pulled up to a stop in front of them, trying to catch enough of a breath to form words.

"What's wrong, Mary?"

What she said stunned them. "They have moved the Lord's body, and I don't know where they have taken him."

"What are you saying?"

"He is just *gone!*"

"Are you sure?"

"I was just there." Her words began pouring out in a panicked rush. "The stone has been rolled back. We looked inside. His body just *is not there!*"

Not real sure what to make of the report, John took off in a dash toward the tomb. John thought his heart might beat out of his chest as he ran. This just didn't make sense.

When he arrived, sure enough, the stone had been rolled back. A little trepidation gripped him, and he stopped short and stood outside of the tomb and peered in. What he saw was absolutely amazing. Where the body should be resting, he could see only an empty shroud laying undisturbed.

Peter finally caught up and didn't stop, rushing right in to the tomb. John followed him in.

What they saw upon closer examination defied all possible explanations. Not only was the shroud laying there in place, but laying separate was the napkin that had been wound around his head, as if it had been neatly folded and laid to the side.

"This doesn't make sense." Peter was trying to figure out. "If they moved his body, *why did they leave his shroud?*"

John's heart was thundering by this time. But there was something else swelling up within him. A realization was beginning to seep into John's thoughts.

"Didn't the Master say something about this?" John tried to piece together. "I thought he was just speaking in parabolic symbols. He had said that he would die and three days later would rise again. You mean this wasn't just a parable? He meant that he would *literally rise from the dead?*"

The despondency that he had been experiencing early in the day was slowly being replaced by a new emotion, rising up and bursting forth into blooms of joy at the realization.

There was just one phrase that could describe it for John. "This is GLORIOUS!"

* * * * *

There is always a path out of the garden. We do not have to live indefinitely in Gethsemane. That would be too much for the human heart to handle. Our God is way too merciful to leave us languishing there.

Our God has marked out a path that leads us out of that place of anguish. By faith we can walk that path. The destination may be unknown, but there is an unseen hand leading us on that way.

The problem is that we want a quick fix. We want instant relief. We always look for an easy out. In a world of "instant gratification," we also want instant answers.

We never have the time to *linger* with God; to try to see what he has in store for us. As much as we hate to admit it, sometimes the human heart gets impatient with God. "*I want an answer, NOW!*" we seem to scream.

It is only after we start walking that path out of Gethsemane that we come to a realization.

The path out may be a long road

It just might be that as you exit Gethsemane you find yourself *in another trial.* It always seems like misfortunes come in groups.

You've heard it said that they come in groups of three. I don't believe it. Sometimes they come in groups of four and five or more.

It is the accumulation of multiple heartaches that can drain your strength and cause you to cry out, "What next? Where is the relief?"

Some of the examples we have used in this book had an instantaneous resolution, such as the immediate transformation of a soul at salvation. Some of the other examples required a long, drawn-out process of recovery.

But even in the instant forgiveness found in salvation, it is the first step in a journey. It is the beginning of a new life; the start of a process of spiritual growth.

In *every* instance, the strength needed is found in the one who knelt in Gethsemane.

The next stop on the path out of Gethsemane was Golgotha. After facing additional trials, we find that we must face *the prospect of death*. It is not necessarily physical death that I am speaking of here. It may be the death of our ambition, or of our selfish pride. It certainly means the death of our will.

To fulfill his mission, his purpose for coming into this world, Jesus had to be in *submission* to the Father. This meant putting aside his own will, his own fears, or anything else that would stand between him and his Father's will.

If we would find God's desire for our life, we too must set our own desires aside. This means putting our will *to death*. The very act of burial means we have put away those things that would hinder us.

In its place, we yield to a greater purpose, a divine purpose, that originates in the heart of God. In so doing, we trust the hand that is able to sustain us in our darkest times.

There is an ultimate destination following that path. When we reach that tomb, something miraculous happens.

Beyond Gethsemane, there is GLORY

Jesus didn't stay dead. He rose again. Death had to relinquish its hold on him. He ascended back to the Father where he sits in majesty and glory! We, too, have that hope. One day, we will rise again and be reunited with those who have died in the Lord's grace.

But what I'm really referring to here is something that happens in this life, and the end result will be glorious. *He is reshaping me;* making me more like him.

I heard a story about a woodcutter, who had fashioned the likeness of a galloping horse out of a block of wood. The skill it took to carve the image would amaze everyone who saw it. It was so lifelike, it looked like it could jump off its stand and run across the room.

One day while someone was admiring it, they had to ask the question, "How were you able to make it look so lifelike? What was the secret? How did you even know where to start?"

The woodcutter replied, "It was simple. I took a block of wood, and cut away everything that didn't look like a horse."

Jesus in speaking to his disciples, made this statement:

It is enough for the disciple that he be as his master, and the servant as his lord. (Matt. 10:25, KJV)

Often what the Lord is doing is chipping away everything that does not resemble our Lord.

I'm not one who tries to claim that I know WHY everything happens in our lives, but I have seen the end result in my life. And I also know that it is a continuing process. I haven't arrived yet, and sometimes I look at myself and think, *There sure is a long way to go.* But he continues to chip away, chip away, chip away in my life.

Because of that, I can make the following statement: *We may not see all that God is doing* with us through these trials. While the Disciples were observing all that Jesus would suffer in Gethsemane, they could not see where it was leading. Their eyes were closed to what God was doing. They did not see that it was God's plan, and that it would lead to the greatest Joy they could imagine.

I know this; *the heartache won't last forever*, and my faith tells me that God is in control and is doing a wonderful work in my life, even if I can't see his hand.

What have you learned through your trial?

I was doing a radio interview concerning the release of my first book *In the Upper Room-Facing the Trial of Your Life*. It was broadcast on Faith Talk Radio out of Atlanta. The hosts, Rick Probst and Dan Ratcliffe, are very good at what they do. They made the interview an interesting conversation, always with a light edge to it.

We were talking about the origin and the main premise of the book. I had written the book while I was going through a particular trial in my life a few years earlier. We covered what had happened during that period and talked about God's faithfulness during the ordeal.

It was toward the end of the interview when Dan asked me this question: "What have you personally learned through this trial?"

So here I am on live radio, trying to put into words all the many things God had taught me during that time. It took me a while to get it all in (most preachers do like to talk), but to the best of my recollection, the following was my answer:

"If I have any *spiritual insight*, it was born out of the trial. Reading old sermon notes can be really eye-opening. You look at something and say, 'Did I *really* say that?' Then again sometimes you come across something insightful that has a deep meaning and you say to yourself, here did that come from?' In thinking back, you realize that it came during a time of trial.

"If I have any *strength to stand*, it was developed during the trial. It's like using a muscle. If you don't use it, it will atrophy. But if you exercise it, it becomes stronger. If you exercise your faith, it becomes stronger. If you're in a position where you have to exercise faith, that's where your strength is developed.

"I've often told people that the person I am was dependent upon three things.

"Number one, the person I have become is due to the work of the grace of God in my heart.

"Number two, the person I have become is due to the way my mom and dad raised me.

"But number three, the person I have become is due to those things I have gone through. They have helped shape me. That's why I say that if I have any strength to stand, they came through the trial.

"It may sound strange to say, but I thank God for the trials, for they have made me who I am.

"And when you get right down to it, my trials are nothing compared to what Jesus suffered *for me*. The one who knelt in Gethsemane, FOR ME. The one who walked up Golgotha, FOR ME. My trials seem small and insignificant by comparison."

This may sound like a repetition of something I have stated in a previous chapter, but it does bear repeating. In fact, it lies at the very heart of the question, "What have you learned during the trial?" How do you face the trial? Can you sense the endgame to your Gethsemane?

Since that interview, I believe I could add two more points to it.

My faith has become stronger since the trials.

Jesus has become more precious to my heart since going through the trial. I have seen his hand at work during the storm. Just thinking about him causes my heart to swell deep inside of me.

Jesus is the one who suffered the agony of Gethsemane for me.

Jesus is the one who bore my sins on the Cross.

Jesus is the God of the empty tomb.

Jesus is the one I run to when my heart is crushed.

Jesus is the "love of my life."

* * * * *

Gradually, the dark clouds once again move to obscure the light from the moon, and the Son of God is hidden from our view.

If you had been standing in Gethsemane that night and had observed this scene, I wonder what would have been going through your mind? Would a tingle have run up your spine in the presence of dark forces? Would you have realized what set this man apart from all others and made him the unique Son of God? Would you have realized the magnitude of the words he prayed and the impact it would have on your life? Would you have realized that because of what transpired here, the world would never be the same?

A more important question would be: what was going through the mind of Christ?

We have tried to examine what was taking place that night. But, the truth is, with our limited vision and inadequate human imagination we cannot even approach the full measure of his agony. How does the mind comprehend the suffering of God?

We have to resort to faith. All things come back to faith.

Here is what I believe.

Jesus was the Son of God, fully God and fully man.

As God, his omniscience could see through the portals of time.

I believe as he knelt there, he could see Peter struggling with his faith.

He could see Del Land struggling for his life.

He could see my Granddaddy struggling with the call to preach.

He could see the young man standing in a hotel room with a gun in one hand and a Gideon Bible in the other.

He could see these things, and he could see the glorious outcome, the *change that would occur in their lives* because of what he would accomplish by going to the cross.

I also believe he could see every one of you who have faced the death of a loved one, and he knew that only HE could remove the sting from death. Only HE could provide sufficient comfort and provide hope as we confront our deepest fear.

Even as he did for me, as I walked through the toughest ordeal in my entire life...

EPILOGUE

Thy rod and thy staff they comfort me.

—Psalm 23:4 (KJV)

Christmas Day, 2016

I'm walking through the house we grew up in. I'm alone with my thoughts. Mom, at ninety-one years of age, is in the hospital with congestive heart failure. She is doing much better now and there is talk of her getting to come home.

So many memories of past Christmases are flooding my mind. Every Christmas Eve, Mom and Dad would host a gathering at this home and invite several family friends over. I would look forward to this almost as much as Christmas morning opening our gifts—almost.

I would go from room to room. There would be Flossie and Granddaddy. I might run into Junior and Mildred Smith. Some years I might see the Clarks, our aunt and uncle and cousins. We would be sipping hot apple cider spiced with cinnamon, admiring our white Christmas tree, and in general just enjoying the holiday season.

At some point during the evening, Johnny would make it around to the Steinway Concert Grand Piano and begin playing some Christmas carols and we would all be singing along. It wouldn't be long before Dad would stand up and begin singing "Beautiful Star of Bethlehem;" his favorite Christmas song.

Dad has been gone for five years now. The night before, after the Christmas Eve service, Johnny, Judy, and I had been getting something to eat at a Huddle House, which has become something of a tradition, and was talking about Dad.

Johnny admits that there are times out of the blue when it all comes back to him and he experiences the raw emotions of that time. I must confess that I do too. There is a part of that you will always carry with you. That is normal.

I thought back to the period following losing Dad. My path out of my Gethsemane had taken a few unexpected turns. It seemed that there was always a "disruption of normal" happening that seemed to stretch on for a few years. During that time, I became a statistic, being unemployed for sixteen months. It was challenging to say the least, but God always provided.

During that time, my relationship with God grew closer and more precious than it had been before. I had loved the Lord ever since he came into my heart, but now there seemed to be a deeper appreciation of his ways.

I had experienced the grace he provided for me. Although my grief was nothing compared to Job's, I could now say as he did, **"I have heard of thee by the hearing of the ear, but now my eye seeth thee"** (Job 42:5, KJV).

It is absolutely true that God is faithful and brought an amazing comfort during our time of grief. I saw a heavenly strength in my Mom, who had been married to Dad for sixty-seven years. It was simply unexplainable.

First of all, the memories of Dad have grown much more precious as time moves on. I remember a young Dad, playing with me as a toddler. I can remember him as my baseball coach, teaching me the intricacies of the game. I remember him taking us to church; our family getting up to sing with Dad taking the lead. All of this brings a warmth and a glow to my heart.

What also brings me comfort is the hope we have in Christ Jesus. For the child of God, this world is not all there is. There is a home that has been prepared for us by the hand of Jesus himself. I know that Dad is experiencing that joy, and that one day there will be a glorious reunion. The thought of that stirs something unexplainable deep within my soul. I can't find another word for it other than GLORIOUS.

That word keeps coming back to my mind, for beyond the suffering there was *glory*. There is the joy in living that God has given to me. There is joy in realizing that no matter how difficult things may be, there is one who went to Gethsemane for me and truly loves me. He followed that path out of the garden to Golgotha and on to a Garden Tomb. Beyond that: GLORY!!!

I walk outside and get in my car to go to the hospital to visit with Mom. As I drive through the near deserted streets this Christmas morning, I think of all the families gathered around the tree; the joy of the young children as they find a world of wonder at the toys left for them. That picture in my mind stirs up the magic in Christmas.

But, in particular this Christmas, what is occupying my mind is the reason we *celebrate*. The birth of the baby who would take the sins of the world and pave the way to an eventual home in heaven. But he also came not just for the future home, but to walk with us in this life. Emmanuel; God with us.

This baby in a manger would one day kneel in a garden called Gethsemane and *bear our griefs and our sorrows* so that we would never bear them alone.

Joy to the world!!!

ABOUT THE AUTHOR

Jimmy Foster is an ordained Baptist minister with over forty-one years in the ministry. He is the author of the book *In the Upper Room: Facing the Trial of Your Life*. He makes his home in the beautiful North Georgia mountains.

CPSIA information can be obtained
at www.ICGtesting.com
Printed in the USA
LVOW08*2302221217
560487LV00001B/2/P